THE

# POOR GENTLEMAN;

A

# *COMEDY,*

IN FIVE ACTS;

AS PERFORMED AT

## The Theatre Royal, Covent Garden.

[FIRST ACTED ON THE 11TH FEBRUARY 1801.]

————————

BY

## GEORGE COLMAN,

*THE YOUNGER.*

————————

## *A NEW EDITION.*

" *Isne tibi melius suadet, qui rem facias ; rem,*
*Si possis, recte : si non quocunque modo rem*
*An qui Fortunæ te responsare superbæ*
*Liberum et erectum præsens hortatur et aptat ?*"     HOR.

————————

London :

PRINTED FOR LONGMAN, HURST, REES, AND ORME,

PATERNOSTER-ROW.

————

1806.

[*Price Two Shillings and Sixpence.*]

1800

JOYCE GOLD, PAINTER, SHOE-LANE.

# PROLOGUE.

WRITTEN BY

*THE HONOURABLE FRANCIS NORTH.*

**A** Long-establish'd Chapman in the trade
Fairly avows he feels himself afraid;
Yet, why should terror in his breast prevail?
He brings the self-same merchandise to sale;
Will his kind Customers their bounty drop,
To the same trader, in a *larger* shop? -
Treat him as you but treated him before;—
Ah! give no less—he *cannot wish* for more.
Thus far the Author has his suit preferr'd;
Now, let the wretched Prologue speak one word.
Unhappy verse! that's calmly doom'd to glide
In mournful silence, down Oblivion's tide;
It swings before the door, an empty sign;
The Play's the treat, the Epilogue's the wine;
While the poor Prologue's dull and formal face
Passes as much unheeded as the *grace*.
Our Bard (the host) prepares, for every guest,
A dish of sentiment, he trusts, well dress'd.
You choose the lighter *entremets* of wit,  [*To the Boxes.*]
Sirloins of solid sense best please the Pit.
You, ye great Gods of this, our little earth,
Love true good humour, season'd high with mirth.
Tho' hard the task, he boldly tries to-night,
To satisfy each various appetite;
Sure to succeed, if *you* approve his plan;
But should you frown——alas! [*Poor Gentleman!*]

## DRAMATIS PERSONÆ.

Lieutenant Worthington     Messrs. MURRAY,
Corporal Foss     - - - KNIGHT.
Sir Charles Cropland    - - H. JOHNSTON,
Warner   -   -   - - DAVENPORT.
Sir Robert Bramble   -   -   - MUNDEN.
Humphrey Dobbings   -   -   - WADDY.
Farmer Harrowby   -   -   - TOWNSEND,
Stephen Harrowby   -   -   - EMERY.
Ollapod   -   -   - FAWCETT,
Frederick   -   -   - LEWIS.

Emily Worthington   -   Mrs. GIBBS.
Miss Lucretia Mac Tab   -   Mrs. MATTOCKS,
Dame Harrowby   -   -   Mrs. POWELL.
Mary   -   -   - Miss SIMS.

Servants, &c.

SCENE—*Kent.*

# THE
# POOR GENTLEMAN.

## ACT I.

### SCENE I.—*A Farm-House Kitchen.*

*Dame* HARROWBY *and* MARY *discovered.*

#### *Dame.*

SURE, my measter won't be worse than his word, and fail to come back, from Lunnun, to-day?

*Mary.* That's what he wo'nt, mother—Feyther be as true as the clock; which, for certain, do go but indifferent, now, seeing it do stand still.

*Farmer* HARROWBY. [*Without.*] Woho! gently wi'em! So, there!

*Dame.* His voice, Mary; warn't it?

*Mary.* I do think so, fegs!—Stay! [*Looks out of the window.*] Dear! here be a new drove of rare horned cattle coming into the yard.

*Dame.* Nay, then, I'll warrant my old man be among 'em.

*Mary.* Yes; there be feyther, as sure as twopence.

*Dame.* Run, Mary! 'tis my measter! run!

[MARY *goes out.*

If I ben't all of a twitter to see my old John Harrowby again!

*Farmer.* [*Without.*] Gently wi'em—So, boys, so!—See 'em well into the yard, Will; and I'll be wi' you, and the rest of the beasts, an' bye.

*Enter* Farmer HARROWBY, MARY *following.*

*Farmer.* Well, mistress!—How am you? Buss! [*Kisses her.*] So—Well, and how am you?

*Dame.* Purely, John, I thank ye! Well, and how?

*Farmer.* Why, I be come from Lunnun, you see—I warrant I smell of smoke like the Nag's-head chimney in the Borough.

*Dame.* And what be the freshest news stirring up at Lunnun, John?

*Farmer.* Freshest news? Why, hops have a heavy sale; wheat and malting samples command a brisk market; new tick beans am risen two shillings per quarter; and white and grey peas keep up to their prices.

*Mary.* Dear! how pleasant 'tis to get the news fresh from Lunnun! La! feyther, if you would but one of those days, now, just carry I up to Lunnun, to learn the genteel fashions at Smithfield and the Borough, and see the modish ladies there a bit!

*Farmer.* No, no, Mary—bide at farm, and know when you am well. But, mistress, let's hear a little all how and about it, at home.

*Dame.* Why, first and foremost, John, our lodgers be come.

*Farmer.* No? you don't say so?

*Mary.* An hour after you left us, feyther.

*Dame.* The old gentleman, Lieutenant Worthington—

*Mary.* And his daughter, Miss Emily;

*Dame.* And his sister-in-law, Madame Lucretia Mac Tab;

*Mary.* And his old soldiering servant, Corporal Foss.

*Farmer.* Whew! fair and softly! One at a time! one at a time!

*Dame.* The Lieutenant be a staid-looking gentleman; and Madame Lucretia——

*Mary.* She be an old maid, feyther; and as frumpish a toad as ever——

*Farmer.* Why, your old maids, for the most part, am but a cross-grain'd kind of cattle—howsomdever, disappointment sours the best of folks.

*Dame.* But Miss be the prettiest little creature——!

*Mary.* And as sweet-temper'd, feyther!

*Farmer.* Be she though?

*Mary.* No more pride nor our Curate. She will fetch a walk with I, in the field, as I go a milking; and speak so kind and so soft! and carry my pail, if I would let her; and all with as much descension and fallibility!

*Farmer.* Bless her heart!

*Stephen.* [*Singing without.*] " There was a regiment of Irish dragoons,"——

*Farmer.* What a dickens! be that son Stephen keeping such a clatter?

*Dame.* Ah! the boy be craz'd, I do think, about soldiering, ever since the Lieutenant's servant, Corporal Foss, have discoursed to him, about champaigning.

*Farmer.* Soldiering! I'll soldier the dog, an' he doesn't stick to plough, wi' a devil to 'un!

*Enter* STEPHEN—*his hair dressed like a soldier's; a black stock, short frock, military spatterdashes; and a carter's whip in his hand.*

*Stephen.* Feyther, you am welcome back to country quarters. Charming weather for the young wheat, feyther.

*Farmer.* Why, you booby, who ha' made thee such a baboon?

*Stephen.* A baboon! he! he! This be milentary, feyther. " Why, Soldiers, why, should we be melancholy, boys?"—[*Singing.*]

*Dame.* The lad's head be crack'd, for certain.

*Stephen.* " Why, Soldiers, why"—— [*Singing.*]

*Farmer.* Crack'd! dang me, but it shall be crack'd an' he don't keep to his business.——

*Stephen.* [*Singing.*]—"Whose business 'tis to die."

*Farmer.* Answer me, you whelp, you! Who have soap'd up and flower'd your numskull after such a fashion?

*Stephen.* Lord, feyther, don't be so vicious. Corporal Foss have put I a little upon drill, that be all.

*Farmer.* Upon drill! and leave the farm to go to rack and manger?

*Stephen.* No, feyther, no. I minds my work, and learns my exercise, all under one. I practise " make " ready, and present," in our bean-field ; and when the Corporal cries " Fire," I shoots the carion crows, as do the mischief.—See, feyther, Corporal Foss have given I this pair of splatterdashes. He wore 'em when he went to beat the Spaniels, at Giberaltar.

*Farmer.* I'll tell thee what. Stephen—I have a great mind to beat thee worse nor e'er a Spaniel was beat i' the world. I'll tire thee of soldiering, I warrant thee.

*Stephen.* [*Singing.*] " The soldier tir'd——

*Mary.* Hush, brother ! you'll scare the whole village.

*Stephen.* [*Singing.*] " With war's alarms."

*Farmer.* Wauns ! let me come at him.

*Dame.* No, John !'

*Mary.* Hold, feyther, hold ! [*Both interfering.*]

*Stephen.* Don't be so hasty, feyther. I minds my business, I tell 'ee. I ha' sow'd three acres of barley before breakfast, already.

*Farmer.* Well, come ; there may be some hope, then, yet. And how did'st sow it, Stephen ?

*Stephen.* I sow'd it to the tune of the Belleisle march. Tol diddle de doll, &c.

*Farmer.* A plough-boy, wi' his hair dress'd, sowing barley to the tune of the Belleisle march !

*Stephen.* Well, I ha' got the team at door, wi' a load of straw, for Squire Tallyho—Woho ! my hearties ! I be a coming to you. Feyther, Corporal says, that our foremost horse, Argus, if he warn't blind, would make a genteel Charger.

*Farmer.* O plague o' the Corporal !

*Stephen.* 'Twould do your heart good to hear him talk, in our chimney corner, about mowing down men, in the field of slaughter. Well, well, I be a going, feyther.—Woho ! old Argus and Jolly there !. The Corporal was wounded, feyther, in the left knee, w' a hand grenadiero——

*Farmer.* Wauns ! an' you don't go, I'll——

*Stephen.* Well, well, I be going. [*Shoulders his*

*whip.*] To the right about, feace ! [*Faces about.*]
" God save great George our King !"
[*Exit, marching and singing.*
*Farmer.* He sha'n't bide on the farm.   I'll turn
him adrift.   I'll——

*Mary.* [*Crying.*] Don't ye, feyther ; don't ye be
so bent against poor Stephen.

*Farmer.* Hoity toity! and you, too ! Why, the
whole house will be turn'd topsy-turvy.

*Mary.* No, indeed, feyther.   Tho' Stephen be a
little upset with the Corporal, nobody shall turn I
topsy-turvy, I do assure you, feyther.
[*A voice without calls—*MARY *!*

*Mary.* There! if that be'nt Miss Emily calling—
Now, do, feyther! do forgive brother Stephen!
Coming, Miss! Now do ye, feyther! Coming ! .
[*Exit* MARY.

*Farmer.* Pretty goings on, truly! Dang it, I wish,
somehow, we had'nt let these lodgers into the house;
—but 'twill help us out with our rent, and—

*Dame.* Ah, John Harrowby! [*Shaking her head.*]

*Farmer.* Why, what now, Deame?

*Dame.* By all I can pick out from the Corporal,
who do love to gossip over his beer, our money be
but in a ticklish way.

*Farmer.* Eh! why, how so?

*Dame.* A desperate poor family, I fancy.

*Farmer.* What, then, the Lieutenant——

*Dame.* Have been in the soldiering line for thirty
long years; but an ugly wound in the arm, which
he got in the wars, beyond sea, have made him unfit for his work any more, it do seem.

*Farmer.* Poor soul!

*Dame.* He be now upon half-pay; which be little
enow, for so many mouths, in one family.

*Farmer.* Poor soul! his landlord in Lunnun, wrote
uncommon well, sure, about his character, and honesty, and so forth.

*Dame.* True, John; but he cou'd stand it, in Lunnun, no longer, you do see.

*Farmer.* Why, look ye, Deame—I didn't, of a

certainty, intend to let our best parlours for nothing: but I wish I may be shot if I can give harsh treatment to an honest man, in misfortune, under my thatch; who have wasted his strength, and his youth, in guarding the land which do give us English farmers a livelihood.

*Dame.* Ah, John! you am at your old kind ways, now!

*Farmer.* Hark! he be opening the parlour door—Leave us together a bit, mistress: I'll speak to 'un, and———

*Dame.* Well, I'll go, John—Ah! bless thy good old heart! I do like to do a good turn myself; but, somehow, my old man do always get the start o' me.                                    [*Exit.*

### Enter WORTHINGTON.

*Farmer.* A good day to you, Sir! [*bowing.*] You am welcome into Kent, Sir,—to my humble cottage, here.

*Worth.* Oh, my landlord, I suppose—Farmer Harrowby?

*Farmer.* Yes, Sir, I be Farmer Harrowby. I hope all things am to your liking at Stocks' Green, Sir—I hope the lodgings, Sir, and my wife, have been agreeable to you, Sir, and so forth.

*Worth.* Nothing can be better. You are well situated here, Mr. Harrowby.

*Farmer.* We am all in the rough, Sir; farmer-like—but the place be well enough for poor folk, Sir.

*Worth.* What does he mean by that? [*Aside.*]

*Farmer.* I be content in my station. There be no reason why a poor man should not be happy.

*Worth.* A million! [*Half aside.*]

*Farmer.* Am there? Well, now, I can't see that: for, putting the case, now, Sir, that you was poor, like I.—

*Worth.* [*Angrily.*] I will not suffer you, Sir, to put a case so familiarly curious.

*Farmer.* Nay, I meant no offence, I'll be sworn, Sir.

*Worth.* But, if you wish to know my sentiments, as far as it may concern yourself, in any money transactions between us, be assured of this—I have too nice a sense of a gentleman's dignity, and too strong a feeling for a poor man's necessity, to permit him to wait a day for a single shilling, which I am indebted to him.

*Farmer.* Dang it! he must be poor; for your great gentry, now-a-days, do pay in a clean contrary fashion. [*Aside.*]

*Worth.* I shall settle with you, for the lodgings, Mr. Harrowby, weekly—One week is due to-day, and—[*Pulling out a purse.*]

*Farmer.* No, Sir, no—under favour, I would like it best quarterly—or half-yearly—or at any long time may suit your conveni——I mean, may suit your pleasure, Sir.

*Worth.* Why so?

*Farmer.* Because—humph—because, Sir—pray, if I may make so bold, Sir, how often may the pay-days come round, with the army-gentlemen, and such like?

*Worth.* Insolent! receive your money, Sir, and let me pass from your apartment. [*Offering it.*]

*Farmer.* Then I wish I may be burnt if I take it now, and that be flat, Sir! [*Rejecting it.*] You am a brave good gentleman, I be told, Sir!—wi a family, and—and—and—in short, there am some little shopmen, of our village, who may press you hard, to settle by the week, pay them greedy ones first, Sir; and if there be enow, at last, left for I, well and good; and if you am inclined for riding, Sir, there be always a gelding at your service, without charge. I be a plain man, Sir; but I do mean nothing but respect; and, so, I humbly wish you a good day, Sir. [*Exit.*

*Worth.* How am I mortified! What has this man heard? Yet, this little simple movement of rustick humanity towards me has—Pshaw! where is my fortitude! Inured to the frowns of the world, one kindly smile of compassion subdues me. Is there a state more galling than to need the decent means of maintaining the appearance which liberal birth, education, and profession demand?—Yes,—yes, there

is an aggravation!—'Tis to have a daughter nursed
in her father's afflictions, with little more to share
with her than the bread of his anguish, the bitter
cup of his sorrows. To see, while I am sinking to
my grave, my friendless, motherless child——Let
me draw a veil over this picture—'Twere not philo-
sophy, but brutality, to look upon it unmoved. I
can not!                                    [*Exit.*

SCENE II.—*An apartment in* Sir CHARLES CROP-
LAND'S *house;* Sir CHARLES CROPLAND *at
breakfast; his Valet de Chambre adjusting his hair.*

*Sir Cha.* Has old Warner, the steward, been told
that I arrived last night?

*Valet.* Yes, Sir Charles; with orders to attend
you this morning.

*Sir Cha.* [*Yawning and stretching.*] What can a
man of fashion do with himself in the country, at
this damn'd dull time of the year!

*Valet.* It is very pleasant, to-day, out in the park,
Sir Charles.

*Sir Cha.* Pleasant, you booby! How can the
country be pleasant in the middle of Spring? All
the world's in London.

*Valet.* I think, somehow, it looks so lively, Sir
Charles, when the corn is coming up.

*Sir Cha.* Blockhead! Vegetation makes the face
of a country look frightful. It spoils hunting. Yet
as my business on my estate, here, is to raise supplies
for my pleasures elsewhere, my journey is a wise one.
What day of the month was it yesterday, when I
left town, on this wise expedition?

*Valet.* The first of April, Sir Charles.

*Sir Cha.* Umph!—When Mr. Warner comes,
show him in.

*Valet.* I shall, Sir Charles.              [*Exit.*

*Sir Cha.* This same lumbering timber upon my
ground has its merits. Trees are notes issued from
the bank of Nature, and as current as those payable
to Abraham Newland. I must get change for a few
oaks, for I want cash consumedly. So, Mr. Warner!

*Enter* WARNER.

*Warner.* Your honour is right welcome into Kent, I am proud to see Sir Charles Cropland on his estate again. I hope you mean to stay on the spot for some time, Sir Charles.

*Sir Cha.* A very tedious time. Three days, Mr. Warner.

*Warner.* Ah, good Sir! things wou'd prosper better if you honour'd us with your presence a little more. I wish you lived entirely upon the estate, Sir Charles.

*Sir Cha.* Thank you, Warner;—but modern men of fashion find it devilish difficult to live upon their estates.

*Warner.* The country about you so charming!

*Sir Ch.* Look ye, Warner—I must hunt in Leicestershire—for that's the thing. In the frosts, and the spring months, I must be in town, at the clubs—for that's the thing. In summer, I must beat the watering places—for that's the thing. Now, Warner, under these circumstances, how is it possible for me to reside upon my estate? For my estate being in Kent——

*Warner.* The most beautiful part of the county.

*Sir Cha.* Curse beauty! we don't mind that in Leicestershire. My estate, I say, being in Kent—

*Warner.* A land of milk and honey!

*Sir Cha.* I hate milk and honey,

*Warner.* A land of fat!—

*Sir Cha.* Damn your fat!—listen to me—my estate being in Kent—

*Warner.* So woody!

*Sir Cha.* Curse the wood! No—that's wrong—for it's convenient. I am come on purpose to cut it.

*Warner.* Ah! I was afraid so! Dice on the table, and, then, the axe to the root! Money lost at play, and then, good lack! the forest groans for it.

*Sir Cha.* But you are not the forest, and why the devil do you groan for it?

*Warner.* I heartily wish, Sir Charles, you may not encumber the goodly estate. Your worthy ancestors had views for their posterity.

*Sir Cha.* And I shall have views for my posterity
—I shall take special care the trees shan't intercept
their prospect.

*Enter* SERVANT.

*Serv.* Mr. Ollapod, the apothecary, is in the hall,
Sir Charles, to inquire after your health.

*Sir Cha.* Show him in.        [*Exit* SERVANT.

The fellow's a character, and treats time as he
does his patients. He shall kill a quarter of an hour
for me, this morning. In short, Mr. Warner, I
must have three thousand pounds in three days.
Fell timber to that amount immediately. 'Tis my
peremptory order, Sir.

*Warner.* I shall obey you, Sir Charles; but 'tis
with a heavy heart! Forgive an old servant of the
family, if he grieves to see you forget some of the
duties for which society has a claim upon you.

*Sir Cha.* What do you mean by duties?

*Warner.* Duties, Sir Charles, which the extrava-
gant man of property can never fulfil—Such as to
support the dignity of an English landholder, for the
honour of old England; to promote the welfare of
his honest tenants; and to succour the industrious
poor, who naturally look up to him for assistance.
But I shall obey you, Sir Charles.        [*Exit.*

*Sir Cha.* A tiresome old blockhead! But where
is this Ollapod? His jumble of physic and shooting
may enliven me—And, to a man of gallantry, in the
country, his intelligence is, by no means, uninterest-
ing, nor his services inconvenient. Ha! Ollapod!

*Enter* OLLAPOD.

*Olla.* Sir Charles, I have the honour to be your
slave. Hope our health is good. Been a hard win-
ter here—Sore throats were plenty; so were wood-
cocks. Flush'd four couple, one morning, in a half-
mile walk, from our town, to cure Mrs. Quarles of
a quinsey. May coming on soon, Sir Charles—
season of delight, love, and campaigning! Hope
you come to sojourn, Sir Charles. Shouldn't be

always on the wing—that's being too flighty. He!
he! he! Do you take, good Sir? do you take?

*Sir Cha.* Oh, yes, I take. But, by the cockade
in your hat, Ollapod, you have added lately, it
seems, to your avocations.

*Olla.* He! he! yes, Sir Charles. I have, now,
the honour to be cornet in the Volunteer Association
Corps of our town. It fell out unexpected—pop
on a sudden; like the going off of a field-piece, or
an alderman in an apoplexy.

*Sir Cha.* Explain.

*Olla.* Happening to be at home—rainy day—no
going out to sport, blister, shoot nor bleed—was
busy behind the counter—You know my shop, Sir
Charles—Galen's head over the door—new-gilt him
last week, by the bye—looks as fresh as a pill.

*Sir Cha.* Well, no more on that head now—
Proceed.

*Olla.* On that Head! he! he! he! That's very
well—very well, indeed! Thank you, good Sir,
I owe you one—Churchwarden Posh, of our town,
being ill of an indigestion, from eating three pounds
of measly pork at a Vestry dinner, I was making
up a cathartick for the patient; when, who should
strut into the shop, but Lieutenant Grains, the
brewer—sleek as a dray horse—in a smart scarlet
jacket, tastily turned up with a rhubarb coloured
lapelle. I confess his figure struck me. I look'd
at him, as I was thumping the mortar, and felt instantly inoculated with a military ardour.

*Sir Cha.* Inoculated! I hope your ardour was
of a favourable sort.

*Olla.* Ha! ha! That's very well—very well, indeed! Thank you, good Sir, I owe you one. We
first talk'd of shooting—He knew my celebrity that
way, Sir Charles. I told him the day before, I had
kill'd six brace of birds—I thumpt on at the mortar
—We then talk'd of physick—I told him, the day
before, I had kill'd—lost, I mean,—sick brace of patients—I thumpt on at the mortar—eyeing him all
the while; for he look'd devilish flashy, to be sure;

and I felt an itching to belong to the Corps. The medical and military both deal in death, you know—so, 'twas natural. He! he!—Do you take, good Sir? do you take?

*Sir Cha.* Take! Oh, no body can miss.

*Olla.* He then talk'd of the Corps itself: said it was sickly; and if a professional person would administer to the health of the Association—dose the men, and drench the horse—he could, perhaps, procure him a Cornetcy.

*Sir Cha.* Well, you jump'd at the offer?

*Olla.* Jump'd! I jump'd over the counter—kick'd down Churchwarden Posh's cathartick into the pocket of Lieutenant Grain's smart scarlet jacket, tastily turn'd up with a rhubarb-coloured lapelle; embraced him and his offer; and I am now Cornet Ollapod, apothecary, at the Galen's-head, of the Association Corps of Cavalry, at your service.

*Sir Cha.* I wish you joy of your appointment. You may now distil water for the shop from the laurels you gather in the field.

*Olla.* Water for—oh! laurel water—he! he! Come, that's very well—very well indeed! Thank you, good Sir, I owe you one. Why, I fancy fame will follow, when the poison of a small mistake I made has ceased to operate.

*Sir Cha.* A mistake?

*Olla.* Having to attend Lady Kitty Carbuncle, on a grand field day, I clapt a pint bottle of her Lady-ship's diet-drink into one of my holsters; intending to proceed to the patient, after the exercise was over. I reach'd the martial ground, and jallop'd—gallop'd! I mean—wheel'd, and flourish'd, with great *eclât*; but when the word "Fire" was given, meaning to pull out my pistol in a hell of a hurry, I presented, neck foremost, the damn'd diet-drink of Lady Kitty Carbuncle; and the medicine being, unfortunately, fermented, by the jolting of my horse, it forced out the cork, with a prodigious pop, full in the face of my gallant Commander.

*Sir Cha.* But, in the midst of so many pursuits, how proceeds practice among the ladies?

*Olla.* He! he! I should be sorry not to feel the pulse of a pretty woman, now and then, Sir Charles. Do you take, good Sir? do you take?

*Sir Cha.* Any new faces, since I left the country?

*Olla.* Nothing worth an item—Nothing new arrived in our town. In the village, to be sure, hard by, a most brilliant beauty has lately given lustre to the lodgings of Farmer Harrowby.

*Sir Cha.* Indeed! is she come-at-able, Ollapod?

*Olla.* Oh no! Full of honour as a Corps of Cavalry; tho', plump as a partridge, 'and mild as emulsion. Miss Emily Worthington, I may venture to say ——

*Sir Cha.* Hey! who? Emily Worthington!

*Olla.* With her father ——

*Sir Cha.* An old officer in the army?

*Olla.* The same.

*Sir Cha.* And a stiff maiden aunt?

*Olla.* Stiff as a ram-rod.

*Sir Cha.* [*Singing and dancing.*] Tol de rol lol!

*Olla.* Bless me! he is seized with St. Vitus's dance.

*Sir Cha.* 'Tis she, by Jupiter! my dear Ollapod! [*Embracing him.*]

*Olla.* Oh, my dear Sir Charles! [*Returning the embrace.*]

*Sir Cha.* The very girl who has just slipt thro' my fingers, in London.

*Olla.* Oho!

*Sir Cha.* You can serve me materially, Ollapod. I know your good nature, in a case like this, and ——

*Olla.* State the symptoms of the case, Sir Charles.

*Sir. Cha.* Oh, common enough. Saw her in London by accident: wheedled the old maiden aunt; kept out of the father's way; followed Emily more than a month,—without success;—and, eight days ago she vanished—there's the outline.

*Olla.* I see no matrimonial symptoms in your case, Sir Charles.

*Sir Cha.* 'Sdeath! do you think me mad? But,

B

introduce yourself to the family, and pave the way
for me. Come! mount your horse—I'll explain
more, as you go to the stable :—but I am in a flame,
in a fever, till I hear further.

*Olla.* In a fever! I'll send you physick enough
to fill a baggage-waggon.

*Sir Cha.* [*Aside.*] So! a long bill as the price of
his politeness!

*Olla.* You need not bleed; but you must have
medicine:

*Sir Cha.* If I must have medicine, Ollapod, I
fancy I shall bleed pretty freely.

*Olla.* He! he! Come, that's very well! very well
indeed! Thank you, good Sir, I owe you one. Before dinner, a strong dose of coloquintida, senna,
scammony, and gambouge ;—

*Sir Cha* Oh, damn scammony and gambouge!

*Olla.* At night a narcotick ;—next day, saline
draughts, camphorated julep, and ————

*Sir Cha.* Zounds! only go, and I'll swallow your
whole shop.

*Olla.* Galen forbid! 'Tis enough to kill every
customer I have in the parish!—Then we'll throw in
the bark—by the bye, talking of bark, Sir Charles,
that Juno of yours is the prettiest pointer bitch——

*Sir Cha.* Well, well, she is yours

*Olla.* My dear Sir Charles! such sport, next
shooting season! If I had but a double barrell'd
gun ——

*Sir Cha.* Take mine that hangs in the hall.

*Olla.* My dear Sir Charles !—Here's a morning's
work! senna and colloquintida—[*Aside.*]

*Sir Cha.* Well, be gone then. [*Pushing him.*]

*Olla.* I'm off—Scammony and gambouge—

*Sir Cha.* Nay, fly man!

*Olla.* I do, Sir Charles—A double barrell'd gun—
I fly—the bark—I'm going—Juno, the bitch—a
narcotick ——

*Sir Cha.* Oh, the devil! [*Pushing him off.*]
　　　　　　　　　　　　　　　　　　　[*Exeunt.*

# ACT II.

## SCENE I.—*The Outside of* Farmer HARROWBY'S *House.*

Farmer HARROWBY, *and* Corporal FOSS.

### FARMER.

WE am not discoursing about your master's bravery, nor his ableness, Mr. Corporal; it be about his goodness, and that like.

*Foss.* A good officer, do you see, can't help being a kind-hearted man; for one of his foremost duties tells him to study the comfort of the poor people below him.

*Farmer.* Dang it, that be the duty of our churchwardens; but many poor people do complain of 'em.

*Foss.* An officer, Mr. Harrowby, isn't a bit like a churchwarden. Ship off an officer, we'll say, with his company, to a foreign climate. He lands, and endures heat, cold, fatigue, hunger, thirst, sickness—Now marching over the burning plain—now up to his knees in wet, in the trench—Now—damn it, Farmer, how can a man suffer such hardships, with a parcel of honest fellows, under his command, and not learn to feel for his fellow-creatures?

*Farmer.* Well; and that be true, sure! And have your master, Lieutenant Worthington, learnt this?

*Foss.* His honour was beloved by the whole regiment. When his wife was shot in his arms, as she lay in his tent—there wasn't a dry eye in our corps.

*Farmer.* Shot in his arms! And was she, though?

*Foss* I never like to think on't, because—Pshaw! [*Wipes his eyes.*] I hate to be unsoldier-like—I whimper'd enough, about it, seventeen years ago.

*Farmer.* Nay, take no shame, Mr. Corporal, take no shame. Honest tears, upon honest faces, am, for all the world, like growing showers upon my meadows—the wet do raise their value.

*Foss.* However, he had something left to console him, after her death.

*Farmer.* And what were that?

*Foss.* 'Twas his child, Mr. Harrowby. Our Miss Emily was then but three years old. I have heard his honour say, her mother had fled to the abode of peace, and left her innocent in the lap of war.

*Farmer.* Pretty soul! she must have been quite scared and frightful.

*Foss.* She didn't know her danger. She little thought, then, that a chance ball might take her father too—and leave her a helpless orphan, in a strange country.

*Farmer.* And, if it had so fell out?

*Foss.* Why, then, perhaps, nothing would have been left her but a poor Corporal, to buckle her on his knapsack: but I would have struggled hard with fortune, to rake up a little pittance for the child of a kind master; whom I had followed through many a campaign, and seen fight his first battle, and his last.

*Farmer.* Do, give us your hand, Mr. Corporal; I'll be shot, now, if I could see an old soldier travelling by, wi' his knapsack, loaded in that manner, and not call him in, to cheer the poor soul, on his journey.

*Foss.* I thank you very kindly, Mr. Harrowby;—but Providence order'd things otherwise: for on the thirteenth of September, in the year eighty-two, a few months after my poor mistress's death, the bursting of a shell, in the garrison, crush'd his honour's arm almost to shivers; and I got wounded on the cap of my knee here. It disabled us both from ever serving again.

*Farmer.* That turn'd out but a baddish day's work, Mr. Corporal.

*Foss.* It turn'd out one of the best day's work, for an Englishman, that ever was seen, Mr. Harrowby! for, on that day, our brave General Elliot gave the Frenchmen and Spaniards as hearty a drubbing, at

Gibraltar, as ever they had in their lives. A true soldier, Mr. Harrowby, would part with all his limbs, and his life after them, rather than Old England should have lost the glory of that day.

*Farmer.* And how long, now, might you lay in your wounds and torments, Mr. Corporal?

*Foss.* 'Twas some time before either of us could be moved: and when we could—being unfit for duty any longer—I follow'd his honour with little Miss Emily, into America, where the war was newly finish'd; for things are cheap there, Mr. Harrowby, and that best suits a Lieutenant's pocket.

*Farmer.* I do fear it do indeed, Mr. Corporal.

*Foss.* But we had a pretty cottage in Canada, on the banks of the river St. Lawrence; shut out from all the world, as I may say.

*Farmer.* Desperate lonesome sure, for soldiers, who am used to be in a bustle.

*Foss.* Why, we soon grew used to it, Mr. Harrowby; and should never have left it, perhaps, if something hadn't call'd his honour, a year ago, into England.

*Farmer.* Well, I must away about the farm—And, do tell your master, Mr. Corporal—tell him gently though, for he be a little touchy like, I do see—that if so be things am cheap in America, they mayn't be found a morsel dearer here, when a wounded English soldier do sit at the door of an English farmer. [*Exit.*

*Enter* STEPHEN.

*Stephen.* [*Singing.*] "Dumbarton's drums beat bonny, O!"—If you am exposed to drill I a bit, Corporal, now be your time.

" I'll stay no more at home,
But I'll follow with the drum." [*Singing.*]

*Foss.* You are back early to-day, my honest lad.

*Steph.* Yes; I do love to be betimes at parade. You'll never find I last comer, when men am to be mustarded! I ha' finished my day's work, out right.

*Foss.* You have lost no time, then.

*Stephen.* No—I ha' lost a cart and horses.

*Foss.* Lost a cart and horses!

*Stephen.* Aye, as good;—for as I were a coming back, empty-handed, wi' our cart, I thought I might as well practise a little, as I walk'd by the side on't —so I held up my head—in the milentary fashion, you do know—and began a marching near foot foremost, to the tune of the British Grenadiers.

*Foss.* Well!

*Stephen.* Dang it! while I ware a carrying my head up, as straight as a hop-pole, our leading horse, blind Argus, drags lean Jolly, wi' the cart at his tail, into a slough.

*Foss.* Zounds! so you plunged the baggage into a morass?

*Stephen.* I don't know what you do call a morass; but they am sticking up to their necks in the mud, at the bottom of Waggon-lodge field.

*Foss.* O fie! you should have look'd to them better.

*Stephen.* Look'd to 'em! Why, how could that possible be, mun, when you teach'd I to hold up my nose to the clouds, like a pig in the wind?

*Olla.* [*Without.*] Here,—Juno!—Juno! Put my pointer into your stable, my lad—Thank ye—if ever you're ill, I'll physick you for nothing.

*Stephen.* Oh, that be Mr. Ollapod, the potter-carrier.

*Enter* OLLAPOD, *with a double-barrell'd gun.*

*Olla.* Stephen, how's your health? Fine weather for the farmers.—Corporal, I've heard of you;— charming Spring for campaigning!—I am Cornet Ollapod, of the Galen's-head; come to pay my respects to your family. Stephen, how's your father, and his hogs, geese, daughter, wife, bullocks, and so forth? Are the partridges beginning to lay yet, Stephen?

*Stephen.* Am you come to shoot the young birds, before they am hath'd, wi' that double barrell'd gun, Mr. Ollapod?

*Olla.* Come, that's very well! very well indeed, for

a bumpkin! Thank you, good Stephen, I owe you half a one. I hope your master, Lieutenant Worthington's well,—whose acquaintance I covet. We soldiers mix together as naturally as medicine in a mortar.

*Foss.* Is your honour in the army then?

*Stephen.* He be only a Coronet in the town corpse.

*Olla.* I wish that lout had a locked jaw! Our association is as fine, and, I may say, without vanity, will be as healthy a Corps, when their spring physick is finished, as any regular regiment in England.

*Foss.* Why, your honour, I have seen a good deal of service in the regular way; and know nothing about Associations; but I think, an' please your honour, if men take up arms to defend their country, they deserve to be thank'd, and respected for it, and it dosn't signify a brass farthing what they are called.

*Olla.* Right—the name's nothing—merit's all—Rhubarb's rhubarb, call it what you will.—Do you take, Corporal? do you take?

*Foss.* I never took any in all my life, an' please your honour.

*Olla.* That's very well, very well indeed! Thank you, Corporal —I owe you one. Now, introduce me to the family.

*Foss.* I can't without orders; and his honour is walk'd out.

*Olla.* That's right; exercise is conducive to health. I'll walk in.

*Foss.* Under favour, your honour, I stand sentinel here; and I can't let a stranger pass, without consulting the garrison. If you please to saunter about for half an hour, I shall speak to our ladies, and——

*Olla.* Well, do so—Stephen, come with me about the grounds.

*Stephen.* I don't like to march wi' you, Mr. Ollapod—You am no regular—Dang me, if I budge wi' him, Corporal, without your word of command.

*Olla.* But, damn it, I'm of the Cavalry.

*Stephen.* No matter for that. You am upon our ground, and unhorsed—Now, Corporal——

*Olla.* Well, if I must. I——

*Foss.* March!

*Stephen.* Come, potter-carrier. Tol de rol.

[*Exeunt* STEPHEN *and* OLLAPOD *at the side.
The Corporal into the house.*

SCENE II.—*A Parlour in* Farmer HARROWBY's
*House.*

*Miss* LUCRETIA MACTAB, *and* EMILY WORTHING-
TON, *discover'd at a table. On the table are work-
boxes, pens, ink, and paper, &c.*—EMILY *at work,*
LUCRETIA *looking over a shabby memorandum book.*

*Luc.* Miss Emily Worthington, you have work'd
those flowers most miserably, child.

*Emily.* Dear, now, I am very sorry for that. I was in
hopes they might have sold for something at London,
that I might have surprised my father with the money.

*Luc.* Sold! Ah, you have none of the proper pride
which my side of the family should have given you—
But, let me look over my expenses since we have been
here. [*Reading.*] "To one week's washing, and
" darning, for the Honourable Miss Lucretia Mac
" Tab, one and sevenpence."—By the bye, Miss
Emily, that sprig of myrtle is thicker than a birch-
broom, and the white rose looks just like a powder-puff.

*Emily.* Indeed! I copied them from nature, grand
aunt.

*Luc.* Grand aunt! you know I hate that hideous
title: but 'tis the fault of your wild American education.

*Emily.* Nay, there can be no fault in that; for
my dear father educated me himself, in our little
cottage, in Canada.

*Luc.* He might have taught you, then, a little
more respect for me, who am of the elevated part
of the family—" Snuff from the chandler, a half-
penny." [*Reading.*]—You know, child, I am your
relation, on your deceased mother's side, of the
noble blood of the Mac Tabs.

*Emily.* Yes, I know that now: but my poor
mother had no relation on her side, when her father,
Lord Lofty, abandon'd her for marrying.

*Luc.* My brother, Lord Lofty, acted as became his rank. You will please to recollect he was one of the oldest barons in Scotland.

*Emily.* Was he, indeed? And you were born only three years after him, grand aunt!

*Luc.* Miss Emily, your ignorance is greater than —— [*Rising.*] I meant, his title is one of the most ancient of the Barony; and he might well be offended at the marriage of my deceased niece, his daughter; for, you know, your father is a mere— but, no matter.

*Emily.* Indeed, but it does matter, though. My father is a gentleman by birth, education, and manners; and that's a character as well deserving respect as the proudest Peer in the realm.

*Luc.* And, pray, what have I insinuated against your father? On the contrary, you might remember how handsomely I have offer'd him my countenance;

*Emily.* I remember it was a year ago that you came, and said you would live with us;—when your brother, Lord Lofty, died so much in debt, and left you destitute.

*Luc.* More shame for him! But didn't I, then, affectionately fly to your father, and tell him I wou'd allow him the honour to maintain me for the future? And hav'n't I, notwithstanding his obscure situation, and narrow finances, kindly lived at the Lieutenant's charge, in the most condescending way in the world?

*Emily.* Condescending!

*Luc.* Yes, Miss Emily; but it seems, by forgetting me, you forget yourself.

*Emily.* No—indeed I know my situation. I am a poor Officer's child: born in the seat of war; rear'd, afterwards, in the wilds of America—rear'd by a kind father, with more cost than his poverty could well bestow. He has dropt, in our retreat, many and many a tear of affection on me; and, as often as I have seen him mourn my mother's loss, I have wonder'd to think that *her* father, in splendour, could be so hard, hearted, while mine, in poverty, was so kind?

*Luc.* Still on the cruelty of your mother's rela-

tions! But, would you be guided by me, Miss Emily,
I wou'd make your fortune. Had you follow'd my
opinion, before we left town, 'relative to Sir Charles
Cropland; as a husband.——

*Emily.* Oh, pray don't mention his name.

*Luc.* And why not, Miss Emily?

*Emily.* Because I am sure he is a libertine.—The
familiar looks he gave me.——

*Luc.* Looks! pshaw! Sir Charles's are the manners, child, of our young men of high fashion.

*Emily.* 'Tis a great pity, then, our young men of
high fashion have so insulting a way of noticing
lowly virtue. A coxcomb that stares humble mo-
desty out of countenance, must be a very cruel coxcomb; and 'tis a sad thing for the heart to be un-
feeling when the head is empty!

*Luc.* Ha! another of your Canada crotchets—
hatch'd on the banks of St. Lawrence; where soli-
tude sits brooding on romance. But will you follow
my counsel?

*Emily.* In respect to Sir Charles Cropland? No—
never. You received his visits without my father's
knowledge. I would not wed the worthiest man
without *his* consent; and he would not command me
to marry the wealthiest, whom I could not esteem.

*Luc.* Pshaw! your father's doctrines, child, have
made him a beggar.

*Emily.* [*With warmth.*] A beggar! no, madam,
he is rich enough to shelter you, who asperse him.

*Luc.* Shelter! shelter, indeed, to a Mac Tab,
who affords him her countenance! I shall acquaint
your father, Miss Emily, with your rudeness to me.

*Emily.* Acquaint him with all, madam. Tell
him, when his daughter hears him misrepresented
by———Tell him———You break my heart, madam
—Tell him what you please.

*Enter* Corporal Foss.

*Foss.* I am come, an' please you, with intelligence
of——What! is my young lady a crying?

*Luc.* Deliver your message, fellow, and ask no
questions.

*Foss.* An' please your ladyship's honour, when an old soldier sees a woman in distress, 'tis to be hoped he may take just half a moment to give her some comfort. Miss Emily!

*Luc.* Blockhead! what excuse has a soldier for half a moment's delay in his business?

*Foss.* The best excuse, an' please you, may be half a moment's charity. A kind commander is loth to punish a poor fellow for doing what heaven rewards. What's the matter, Miss Emily? [*Going to her.*]

*Emily.* 'Tis nothing, good Corporal—lead me to the door of my chamber. [*Corporal is going with her.*]

*Luc.* You may be taught your duty to me better, Sir.

*Foss.* I humbly beg pardon; but my first duty, in these quarters, is to my master and his child; I know that as a servant. My second is, to a woman in grief;—I am sure of that as a man. My third is to your ladyship's honour; and I'll be back to perform it, in as quick a march as a cripple can make of it. Come, Miss Emily, come!

[*Exit, leading* EMILY.

*Luc.* Provoking! a stupid, technical, old—— But what can a woman of birth expect—when the ducks waddle into her drawing-room, and her groom of the chambers is a lame soldier of foot!

*Re-enter* Foss.

*Foss.* There is one Mr. Ollapod at the gate, an' please your ladyship's honour, come to pay a visit to the family.

*Luc.* Ollapod? What is the gentleman?

*Foss.* He says he's a Cornet in the Galen's-head. 'Tis the first time I ever heard of the Corps.

*Luc.* Ha,—some new-rais'd regiment. Show the gentleman in. [*Exit Foss.*

The country, then, has heard of my arrival, at last. A woman of condition, in a family, can never long conceal her retreat. Ollapod! that sounds like an ancient name. If I am not mistaken, he is nobly descended.

*Enter* OLLAPOD.

*Olla.* Madam, I have the honour of paying my respects. Sweet spot, here, among the cows;—good for consumptions—Charming woods hereabouts—Pheasants flourish—so do agues—Sorry not to see the good Lieutenant—admire his room——hope, soon, to have his company. Do you take, good madam? do you take?

*Luc.* I beg, Sir, you will be seated.

*Olla.* Oh, dear madam! [*Sitting down.*] A charming chair to bleed in? [*Aside.*

*Luc.* I am sorrow Mr. Worthington is not at home, to receive you, Sir.

*Olla.* You are a relation of the Lieutenant, madam?

*Luc.* I! only by his marriage, I assure you, Sir. Aunt to his deceased wife: but I am not surprised at your question. My friends, in town, would wonder to see the Honourable Miss Lucretia MacTab, sister to the late Lord Lofty, coop'd up in a farm-house.

*Olla.* [*Aside.*] The honourable! humph! a bit of quality tumbled into decay—The sister of a dead Peer in a pig-stye!

*Luc.* You are of the military, I am informed, Sir.

*Olla.* He! he! yes, madam. Cornet Ollapod, of our Volunteers—a fine healthy troop—ready to give the enemy a dose, whenever they dare to attack us.

*Luc.* I was always prodigiously partial to the military. My great grandfather, Marmaduke, Baron Lofty, commanded a troop of horse under the Duke of Marlborough, that famous general of his age.

*Olla.* Marlborough was a hero of a man, madam; and lived at Woodstock—a sweet sporting country; where Rosamond perish'd by poison—Arsenick, as likely as any thing.

*Luc.* And have you served much, Mr. Ollapod?

*Olla.* He! he! Yes, Madam—served all the nobility, and gentry, for five miles round.

*Luc.* Sir!

*Olla.* And shall be happy to serve the good Lieutenant and his family. [*Bowing.*]

*Luc.* We shall be proud of your acquaintance, Sir. A gentleman of the army is always an acquisition, among the Goths and Vandals of the country; where every sheepish Squire has the air of an apothecary.

*Olla.* Madam! An apothe——Zouns!—hum!— He! he! I—You must know, I——I deal a little in Galenicals, myself. [*Sheepishly.*]

*Luc.* Galenicals! Oh, they are for operations, I suppose, among the military.

*Olla.* Operations! He! he! Come, that's very well; very well indeed! Thank you, good Madam, I owe you one. Galenicals, Madam, are medicines.

*Luc.* Medicines!

*Olla.* Yes, physick: buckthorn, senna, and so forth.

*Luc.* [*Rising.*] Why, then, you are an apothecary!

*Olla.* [*Rising too, and bowing.*] A man-midwife, at your service, Madam.

*Luc.* At my service indeed!

*Olla.* Yes, Madam! Cornet Ollapod, at the gilt Galen's-head, of the volunteer Association Corps of Cavalry—As ready for the foe, as a customer: always willing to charge them both—Do you take, good Madam? do you take?

*Luc.* And has the Honourable Miss Lucretia Mac Tab been talking, all this while, to a petty dealer in drugs?

*Olla.* Drugs! 'dam'me, she turns up her honourable nose, as if she was going to swallow them! No man more respected than myself, Madam. Courted by the Corps, idolized by invalids; and for a shot —ask my friend, Sir Charles Cropland.

*Luc.* Is Sir Charles Cropland a friend of yours, Sir?

*Olla.* Intimate. He doesn't make wry faces at physick, whatever others may do, Madam. This village flanks the intrenchments of his park—full of fine fat venison; which is as light a food for digestion as——.

*Luc.* But he is never on his estate here, I am told.

*Olla.* He quarters there at this moment.

*Luc.* Bless me! Has Sir Charles, then——?

*Oll.* Told me all—your accidental meeting in the

metropolis, and his visits when the Lieutenant was out.

*Luc.* Oh, shocking! I declare I shall faint.

*Olla.* Faint! never mind that, with a medical man in the room—I can bring you about, in a twinkling.

*Luc.* And what has Sir Charles Cropland presumed to advance about me?

*Olla.* Oh, nothing derogatory. Respectful as a duck legg'd drummer to a commander in chief.

*Luc.* I have only proceeded, in this affair, from the purest motives; and in a mode becoming a Mac Tab.

*Olla.* None dare to doubt it.

*Luc.* And, if Sir Charles has dropt in, to a dish of tea, with myself and Emily, in London, when the Lieutenant was out, I see no harm in it.

*Olla.* Nor I, neither:—except that tea shakes the nervous system to shatters. But, to the point; the Baronet's my bosom friend—Having heard you were here, "Ollapod," says he, squeezing my hand in his own, which had strong symptoms of fever, "Ollapod," says he, "you are a military man, and may be trusted."—"I'm a Cornet," says I, "and close as a pill-box"—"Fly, then, to Miss Lucretia Mac Tab, that honourable picture of prudence."—

*Luc.* He! he! did Sir Charles say that?

*Olla.* [*Aside.*] How these tabbies love to be toaded!

*Luc.* In short, Sir Charles, I perceive, has appointed you his emissary, to consult with me when he may have an interview.

*Olla.* Madam, you are the sharpest shot at the truth I ever met in my life. And, now we are in consultation, what think you of a walk with Miss Emily, by the old elms, at the back of the village, this evening?

*Luc.* Why, I am willing to take any steps which may promote Emily's future welfare.

*Olla.* Take steps! what, in a walk? He! he! come, that's very well; very well indeed! Thank you, good Madam; I owe you one. I shall communicate to my friend, with due dispatch. Command Cornet Ollapod on all occasions, and whatever the gilt Galen's-head can produce.——

*Luc.* [*Curtseying*] Oh, Sir!

*Olla.* By the bye, I have some double distill'd lavender water, much admired in our Corps. Permit me to send a pint bottle by way of present.

*Luc.* Dear Sir, I shall rob you.

*Olla.* Quite the contrary:—For I'll set it down to Sir Charles as a quart. [*Aside.*] Madam, your slave. You have prescribed for our patient like an able physician.—Not a step.

*Luc.* Nay, I insist——

*Olla.* Then I must follow in the rear. The physician always before the apothecary.

*Luc.* Apothecary! Sir, in this business, I look upon you as a general officer.

*Olla.* Do you? Thank you, good-Ma'am: I owe you one. [*Exeunt.*

---

## ACT III.

### SCENE I. *An Apartment in Sir* ROBERT BRAMBLE's *House.*

*Sir* ROBERT BRAMBLE, *and* HUMPHREY DOBBINS.

#### *Sir* ROBERT.

I TELL you what, Humphrey Dobbins; there isn't a syllable of sense in all you have been saying. But I suppose you will maintain that there is.

*Dob.* Yes.

*Sir Rob.* Yes! is that the way you talk to me, you old boar? What's my name?

*Dob.* Robert Bramble.

*Sir Rob.* A'n't I a Baronet? Sir Robert Bramble, at Blackberry Hall, in the county of Kent? 'Tis time you should know it; for you have been my clumsy, two fisted valet de chambre, these thirty years—Can you deny that?

*Dob.* Humph!

*Sir Rob.* Humph! what the devil do you mean by

humph? Open the rusty door of your mouth, and make your ugly voice walk out of it. Why don't you answer my question?

*Dob.* Because, if I contradicted you there, I should tell a lie ; and, whenever I agree with you, you are sure to fall out.

*Sir Rob.* Humphrey Dobbins—I have been so long endeavouring to beat a few brains into your pate, that all your hair has tumbled of it, before I can carry my point.

*Dob.* What, then? Our Parson says, my head is an emblem of both our honours.

*Sir Rob.* Aye, because honours, like your head, are apt to be empty.

*Dob.* No ;—but if a servant has grown bald under his master's nose, it looks as if there was honesty on one side, and regard for it on t'other.

*Sir Rob.* Why, to be sure, old Humphrey, you are as honest a———. Pshaw ! the parson means to palaver us !—but, to return to my position,—I tell you I don't like your flat contradiction.

*Dob.* Yes, you do.

*Sir Rob.* I tell you I don't. I only love to hear men's arguments, and I hate their flummery.

*Dob.* What do you call flummery ?

*Sir Rob.* Flattery, you blockhead ! A dish too often served up, by a paltry poor man, to paltry rich ones.

*Dob.* I never serve it up to you. -

*Sir Rob.* No, I'll be sworn. You give me a dish of a different description.

*Dob.* Umph ! what is it ?

*Sir Rob.* Sour krout, you old crab.

*Dob.* I have held you a stout tug at argument this many a year.

*Sir Rob.* And yet I could never teach you a syllogism. Now, mind ; when a poor man assents to what a rich man says, I suspect he means to flatter him. Now I am rich, and hate flattery—*Ergo,—* when a poor man subscribes to my opinion, I hate him.

*Dob.* That's wrong.

*Sir Rob.* Very well—*Negatur.* Now prove it.

*Dob.* Put the case so, then—I am a poor man——.

*Sir Rob.* You lie, you scoundrel! You know you shall never want while I have a shilling.

*Dob.* Bless you!

*Sir Rob.* Pshaw! proceed.

*Dob.* Well, then, I am a poor——I must be a poor man, now, or I shall never get on.

*Sir. Rob.* Well, get on. *Be* a poor man.

*Dob.* I am a poor man; and I argue with you, and convince you you are wrong—then you call yourself a blockhead, and I am of your opinion: Now, that's no flattery.

*Sir Rob.* Why, no: but, when a man's of the same opinion with me, he puts an end to the argument; and that puts an end to conversation:—So, I hate him for that. But where's my nephew, Frederick?

*Dob.* Been out these two hours.

*Sir Rob.* An undutiful cub!—Only arrived from Russia last night; and, though I told him to stay at home till I rose, he's scampering over the fields, like a Calmuc Tartar.

*Dob.* He's a fine fellow.

*Sir Rob.* He *has* a touch of our family. Don't you think he's a little like me, Humphrey?

*Dob.* Bless you, not a bit. You are as ugly an old man as ever I clapt my eyes on.

*Sir Rob.* Now, that's damn'd impudent! But there's no flattery in it; and it keeps up the independence of argument. His father, my brother, Job, is of as tame a spirit! Humphrey, you remember my brother Job?

*Dob.* Yes; you drove him to Russia, five-and-twenty years ago.

*Sir Rob.* I drove him! [*Angrily.*]

*Dob.* Yes, you did—You wou'd never let him be at peace, in the way of argument.

*Sir Rob.* At peace! Zounds! he would never go to war.

*Dob.* He had the merit to be calm.

*Sir Rob.* So has a duck-pond. He was a bit of

c

still life; a chip; weak water-gruel; a tame rabbit, boil'd to rags, without sauce or salt. He received men's arguments with his mouth open, like a poor's box gaping for halfpence; and, good or bad, he swallow'd them all, without any resistance. We cou'dn't disagree, and so we parted.

*Dob.* And the poor meek gentleman went to Russia, for a quiet life.

*Sir Rob.* A quiet life! Why, he married the moment he got there. Tack'd himself to the shrew relict of a Russian merchant; and continued a speculation with her, in furs, flax, pot-ashes, tallow, linen, and leather. And what's the consequence? thirteen months ago he broke.

*Dob.* Poor soul! his wife should have follow'd the business for him.

*Sir Rob.* I fancy she did follow it; for she died just as it went to the devil. And now, this madcap, Frederick, is sent over to me for protection. Poor Job! now he's in distress, I mustn't neglect his son.

[FREDERICK *is heard, singing, without.*

*Dob.* Here comes his son—That's Mr. Frederick.

*Enter* FREDERICK.

*Fred.* Ah, my dear uncle! good morning. Your park is nothing but beauty.

*Sir Rob.* Who bid you caper over my beauty? I told you to stay in doors, till I got up.

*Fred.* Eh? Egad so you did! I had as entirely forgot it, as ———

*Sir Rob.* And pray what made you forget it?

*Fred.* The sun.

*Sir Rob.* The sun! He's mad. You mean the moon, I believe.

*Fred.* Oh, my dear Sir, you don't know the effect of a fine Spring morning upon a young fellow just arrived from Russia. The day look'd bright; trees budding; birds singing; the park was gay; so, egad, I took a hop, step, and a jump, out of your old balcony; made your deer fly before me like the wind; and chased them all round the park, to get an appetite, while you were snoring in bed, uncle.

*Sir Rob.* Ah! so the effect of English sun, upon a young Russian, is to make him jump out of a balcony, and worry my deer.

*Fred.* I confess it had that influence upon me.

*Sir Rob.* You had better be influenced by a rich old uncle; unless you think the sun likely to leave you a fat legacy.

*Fred.* Sir, I hate fat legacies.

*Sir Rob.* Sir, that's mighty singular.  They are pretty solid tokens of kindness, at least.

*Fred.* Very melancholy tokens, uncle—They are the posthumous dispatches Affection sends to Gratitude, to inform us we have lost a generous friend.

*Sir Rob.* How charmingly the dog argues!

*Fred.* But, I own my spirits ran away with me, this morning.   I will obey you better in future; for they tell me you are a very worthy, good sort of old gentleman.

*Sir Rob.* Now, who had the familiar impudence to tell you that?

*Fred.* Old rusty, there.

*Sir Rob.* Why, Humphrey, you didn't?

*Dob.* Yes, but I did, tho'.

*Fred.* Yes, he did; and, on that score I shall be anxious to sohw you obedience: for, 'tis as meritorious to attempt sharing in a good man's heart, as it is paltry to have designs upon a rich man's money. A noble nature aims its attentions full breast high, uncle; a mean mind levels its dirty assiduities at the pocket.

*Sir Rob.* [*Embracing him.*]   Jump out of every window I have in my house! Hunt my deer into high fevers, my fine fellow! ay, damn it! this is spunk, and plain speaking! Give me a man, who is always plumping his dissent to my doctrines smack in my teeth.

*Fred.* I disagree with you there, uncle!

*Dob.* So do I.

*Fred.* You! you forward puppy! if you were not so old, I'd knock you down.

*Sir Rob.* I'll knock you down, if you do. I won't

c 2

have, my servants thump'd into dumb flattery. I won't let you teach 'em to make Silence a toad-eater.

*Dob.* Come, you're ruffled—Let's go to the business of the morning.

*Sir Rob.* Damn the business of the morning! Don't you see we are engaged in discussion? I hate the business of the morning.

*Dob.* No, you don't.

*Sir Rob.* And why not?

*Dob.* Because 'tis charity.

*Sir Rob.* Pshaw! damn it—! well—we mustn't neglect business—If there be any distresses in the parish, read the morning list, Humphrey.

*Dob.* [*Reading.*] Jonathan Huggins, of Muck Mead, is put into prison.

*Sir Rob.* Why, 'twas but last week Gripe, the attorney, recovered two cottages for him, by law, worth sixty pounds.

*Dob.* And charged a hundred and ten for his trouble!—So, seiz'd the cottages, for part of his bill, and threw Jonathan in jail, for the remainder.

*Sir Rob.* A harpy! I must relieve the poor fellow's distress.

*Fred.* And I must kick his attorney.

*Dob.* The Curate's horse is dead.

*Sir Rob.* Pshaw! there's no distress in that.

*Dob.* Yes, there is—to a man who must go twenty miles, every Sunday, to preach three sermons, for thirty pounds a year.

*Sir Rob.* Why won't Punmock, the vicar, give him another nag?

*Dob.* Because 'tis cheaper to get another curate ready mounted.

*Sir Rob.* What's the name of the black pad I purchased last Tuesday, at Tunbridge?

*Dob.* Belzebub.

*Sir Rob.* Send Belzebub to the Curate, and tell him to work him, as long as he lives.

*Fred.* And, if you have a tumble down tit, send him to the vicar, to give him a chance of breaking his neck.

*Sir Rob.* What else?

*Dob.* Somewhat out of the common. There's one Lieutenant Worthington, a disabled officer, and a widower, come to lodge at Farmer Harrowby's in the village. He's plaguy poor indeed, it seems: but more proud than poor, and more honest than proud.

*Fred.* That sounds like a noble character!

*Sir Rob.* And so he sends to me for assistance?

*Dob.* He'd see you hang'd first. Harrowby says, he'd sooner die than ask any man for a shilling. There's his daughter, and his dead wife's aunt, and an old corporal, that has served in the wars with him —he keeps them all upon his half-pay.

*Sir Rob.* Starves them all, I am afraid, Humphrey.

*Fred.* [*Going.*] Uncle, good morning!

*Sir Rob.* Where the devil are you running, now?

*Fred.* To talk to Lieutenant Worthington.

*Sir Rob.* And what may you be going to say to him?

*Fred.* I can't tell till I encounter him; and then, uncle, when I have an old gentleman by the hand, who is disabled in his country's service, and struggling to support his motherless child, a poor relation, and a faithful servant, in honourable indigence,—impulse will supply me with words to express my sentiments. [*Hurrying away.*]

*Sir Rob.* Stop, you rogue! I must be before you, in this business.

*Fred.* That depends upon who can run fastest. So, start fair, uncle! and here goes! [*Runs out.*]

*Sir Rob.* Stop! Why, Frederick!—A jacka-napes!—To take my department out of my hands! I'll disinherit the dog for his assurance.

*Dob.* No, you won't.

*Sir Rob.* Won't I? dam'me, if I———But we'll argue that point as we go. Come along, Humphrey!

[*Exeunt.*

SCENE II.—*The Front of* Farmer HARROWBY'S
*House.*

Corporal Foss *crossing the stage,* STEPHEN
*following him.*

*Stephen.* [*Calling.*] Hollo! I say, Mr. Corporal!

*Foss.* Ah! master Stephen! is it you?

*Stephen.* What do you think I ha' been about?

*Foss.* Getting the cart and horses out of the mud,
I suppose.

*Stephen.* No, feyther's head man be gone to dex-
tricate the cattle: but you was telling I, t'other day,
you do know, about a springing up of a mine; which
be done by a man, they do call a pye on an ear.

*Foss.* A Pioneer is our name for it, my honest lad.
Aye, I have seen some of that work, in my day,
master Stephen! If we could get but a little spot of
ground, now, with a bit of good-for-nothing build-
ing upon it.——

*Stephen.* I ha' found out just such a place, Mr.
Corporal.

*Foss.* Then I'll show you the whole process.

*Stephen.* I ha' done the whole progress myself.

*Foss.* Have you?

*Stephen.* You do know feyther's pig-stye?

*Foss.* Yes;—It stands on the edge of the dry
ditch, at the back of the house.

*Stephen.* That's where it did use to stand, sure
enow—But I ha' blow'd it up wi' gunpowder.

*Foss.* The devil you have! and how?

*Stephen.* All according to rule, mun;—just as you
laid it down. I bored a hole under the ditch, wi' the
peel of our oven; and then I laid in my bumbustibles.

*Foss.* Well?

*Stephen.* Why, I clapt the kitchen poker to un,
red hot; and it all went up wi' a desperate complo-
sion, just as you destroy'd that outlandish buttery.

*Foss.* Bless us, master Stephen! then you have
ruined the town, in cold blood, and kill'd all the
inhabitants.

*Stephen.* No: the inhabitants am lying in the ditch,

as pert as daisies—only the little pigs am singed quite bald, and the ould white sow be as black as the devil.

*Enter* MARY.

*Mary.* Brother Stephen! Come here brother Stephen. Feyther do vow vengeance again ye. If you do go on o' this fashion, what will the neigh-bours call ye, Stephen?

*Stephen.* Call me? why, a perspiring young hero, of five foot six inches, willing to mortalize himself, in the field of March.

WORTHINGTON *crosses the Stage, and goes into the House.*

*Foss.* There—his honour is come home—I must go in for orders.

*Mary.* Oh, Mr. Corporal, Joe Shambles, the butcher's boy, ha' brought this from our town, for your master. [*Giving a letter.*]

*Foss.* One letter. Is this all he left for us, my pretty maid?

*Mary.* No; he left a leg of mutton.

*Foss.* Oh. [*Goes in.*]

*Stephen.* How stately Mr. Corporal do march, surely! he be as upright as our gander. Come, Mary! afore feyther do come home, lets you and I go wash the gunpowder pigs.

*Mary.* How, Stephen?

*Stephen.* We'll go to the dairy, and chuck 'em into the milk pails.

[*Voice without.*] Stephen!

*Stephen.* Wauns! there be feyther! Run, Mary, run! [*Exeunt.*

SCENE III. *The Parlour, in* HARROWBY's *House.*

*Enter* WORTHINGTON *and the* CORPORAL.

*Worth.* Where are the ladies, Corporal?

*Foss.* They are gone to take a walk, an' please your honour.

*Worth.* Oh!—[*Sitting down.*]—Mine has some-what fatigued me.

*Foss.* Under favour, I think your honour takes too

much exercise—it always brings on the torment in your wound again.

*Worth.* You bustle about for me more than I could wish, Corporal. You got your wound in an ugly place, you know.

*Foss.* I got it at Gibraltar; the same ugly place with your honour—That cursed shell struck us both together.

*Worth.* I remember it did, Corporal. [*Sighing.*]

*Foss.* And, when I lay on the ground, and your honour's left arm was so terribly wounded, you stretch'd out your right to help me.

*Worth.* I don't remember that, Corporal.

*Foss.* [*Warmly.*] Don't you? but I do—and I wish I may be damn'd if ever I forget it.

*Worth.* Well, well—do not let us swear about it, Corporal.

*Foss.* I hate swearing, your honour, as much as our Chaplain loved brandy; but when a man's heart's too full, I fancy, somehow, there's an oath at the top on't; and when that pops out, he's easy! Ah! we had warm work that day, your honour!

*Worth.* We had, indeed, Corporal.

*Foss.* There was Crillon's batteries, and four thousand men behind us at land.

*Worth.* Moreno, with his Fleet, before us at sea.

*Foss.* At ten in the morning, the Spanish Admiral began his cannonade.

*Worth.* Our battery from the King's bastion open'd directly.

*Foss.* Red-hot shot poured from the garrison.

*Worth.* Cannons roar!

*Foss.* Mortars and howitzers!

*Worth.* The enemy's shipping in flames!

*Foss.* Fire again!

*Worth.* They burn!

*Foss.* They blow up!

*Worth.* They sink.

*Foss.* Victory! Old England for ever, your honour! Huzza!

*Worth.* Ay, Corporal; against the world in arms, Old England for ever.

*Both.* Huzza!

*Foss.* [*After a pause, gravely.*] We have no limbs to help our country, now. We shall never fight for Old England again, your honour.

*Worth.* [*Mournfully.*] No, Corporal! 'tis impossible!

*Foss.* But our *hearts* are for our country still. Tho' your honour has only half-pay, and I am but an out-pensioner of Chelsea.

*Worth.* We have no right to complain, Corporal. National bounty, beyond its limits, would be national waste; and 'tis impossible to provide sumptuously for all.

*Foss.* That's true, your honour. Every hero, that loses his life in the field, must not expect a marvel monument.

*Worth.* 'Tis of little import, Corporal—A gallant Soldier's memory will flourish, though humble turf be osier bound upon his grave. The tears of his Country will moisten it; and vigorous laurel sprout among the cypress that shadows his remains. But 'tis a bitter thought, when we must depart, to leave, unprotected, the few who are joined with us, in the ties of affection, and the bonds of nature!

*Foss.* Your honour is joined in no bond with any body, but Mr. Burford, for five hundred pounds.

*Worth.* [*Smiling.*] I did not mean that, Corporal. There, however, I am easy. My friend has strict honour: and, should he die, the regular insurance of his life secures me from injury, in lending him my name. But 'tis strange I have not heard from him.

*Foss.* I had forgot—Here is a letter just brought for your honour. [*Gives it.*]

*Worth.* Let me see—[*Opening it.*] "Tunbridge" —Tis written in the neighbouring town—who should know me there? [*Reads.*]

"Sir,

"I am instructed by Mr. Ferret, solicitor of London, to inform you, that Mr. Burford died on

" the 26th ultimo, on his way to the Insurance office;
" whereby the Policy, which had expired the day be-
" fore, is become void, and the Bond, and Warrant
" of attorney for 500*l*. remain in force against you.
" If the money be not paid, forthwith, I shall enter
" up judgment, instantly, for the recovery of the
" same."

My child! my child!

*Foss.* Your honour!

*Worth.* Ruin'd past hope!

*Foss.* [*Stepping up to him.*] Don't say that, your
honour; for while your half-pay continues——

*Worth.* My creditor will grasp all—My person
seized, and my poor child destitute!

*Foss.* Destitute! what, my young mistress?—
and you?—and —— don't give way to grief, your
honour. I am lame, to be sure, but I am fit for la-
bour still—There's my little pension, too, from Chelsea—Things may come about; and till they do,
you and my young mistress shall never know want,
while the old Corporal has a limb left to work, or a
penny in his pocket.

*Worth.* Corporal, I——

*Enter* FREDERICK.

*Fred.* Yes, this is he! Zounds! I am quite out
of breath—Sir, I am come to—Whew! I beg pardon—but, as you perceive, I am devilishly blown.

*Worth.* Leave us, Corporal.        [*Exit* Foss.
At your leisure, Sir, I should be glad to know
whom I have the honour of addressing.

*Fred.* I am Frederick Bramble, Sir. My uncle,
Sir Robert Bramble, lives at the foot of this infernal
hill. He fix'd his house there, I fancy, for the sake
of argument; because most men maintain it is bad
to build in a bottom. He is as charitable as a Chris-
tian, Sir, and as rich as a Jew.

*Worth.* I give you joy of a relation, Sir, who has
so much virtue, with so much wealth. When Fortune enriches the benevolent, the Goddess removes
the bandage from her brow, that she may bestow a

gift with her eyes open. But as I am a stranger here, and a recluse, I have no right to enter further into your uncle's character.

*Fred.* Yet he has just now, Sir, taken a right to enter into yours.

*Worth.* May he not rather have taken a liberty, Sir?

*Fred.* 'Tis his duty to be the most inquisitive fellow in the neighbourhood.

*Worth.* 'Tis a strange duty for a gentleman!

*Fred.* I hope not, in this country, Sir. If a gentleman be in the commission of the peace, and living on his own estate, he should be anxious, I think, to inquire into the conduct of those around him, that he may distribute justice as a magistrate, and kindness as a man.

*Worth.* But how can your uncle's principle apply to me, Sir? A secluded sojourner, with a quiet family, lodging with one of his tenants?

*Fred.* Why, he has heard of the ——hem!—— that is, I mean —— the —— peculiarity of your situation ——

*Worth.* [*Haughtily.*] Sir?

*Fred.* I shall make a bungling business of this after all! [*Aside.*]—I say, Sir, that my uncle, as I told you, is a warm old heart, who busies himself in learning the circumstances of every body about him, and ————

*Worth.* The circumstances!

*Fred.* Yes; and so Humphrey Dobbins,—a stupid old servant,—among other intelligence this morning, happened to—to mention you, and —— damn it, Sir, the truth's the truth:—I ran here to prevent my uncle's offering his assistance too bluntly, and I fear I have done it too bluntly, myself.

*Worth.* It wou'd be absurd, Sir, to affect blindness to the motives of your visit—I see them clearly, and thank you cordially. You have touch'd the heart of a veteran soldier; but go no farther; if you proceed, you will wound the dignity of a gentleman.

*Fred.* I came here to heal wounds; by my soul I did! 'Tis not in my nature to inflict them. I am

new in England; ignorant in the manners of the
country—for I arrived here, last night, from Russia,
where I was born; but surely, surely, it cannot be
offensive, in any part of the globe, to tell the afflicted
we feel for them.    Pray, give me your hand !

*Worth.*  Take it, Sir, take it.  Receive the grasp
of gratitude, and be gone.

*Fred.*  Not till you first permit me to ——

*Worth.*  I can accept no favours, of the nature you
offer, where I have no claim: and what claim, young
man, can I have upon your attentions ?

*Fred.*  The claim each man has, in common, upon
his fellow.  We are all passengers on life's highway;
and when a traveller sticks in the mire, on the road,
the next that comes by is a brute who doesn't stretch
out a hand, to extricate him.

*Worth.*  That may hold in the courtesies of life;
but I do not admit it as an argument in essentials.

*Fred.*  Then, I wish my uncle were here, with all
my heart, Sir; he'd argue this point with you, or
any other, to all eternity.

*Worth.*  I want no arguments upon points of honour.
Honour, the offspring of honesty, dictates for itself.

*Fred.*  Sir, I respect it, for its parent's sake; tho'
the child is a little maddish : for Honour is, sometimes, cutting throats, where Honesty would be
shaking hands.    But let me entreat you to relax—
to be persuaded.    Come, my dear Sir ! true honour,
I trust, can never have reason to blush, because
honesty is assisted.

*Worth.*  [*After a pause*]  You have burst upon
me at a critical, a trying moment.  I have a family ; a
beloved child, from whom I may be shortly torn,
without the means of —— No matter.    Even the
griefs that, inwardly, wring me, would not force me
to unbend, were there not a native ingenuousness in
your manner, which wins me.    To you, then, to a
youthful stranger, whose sympathy comes o'er a rug-
ged soldier's nature, as pictur'd Love bestrides the
lion, to you I will owe a temporary obligation.

*Fred.*  Will you? Then you have made me the

happiest dog that—[*Feeling his pockets.*] Eh?—no
—no, zounds—! I mean, Sir, you have made me
look like the silliest dog in the world!

*Worth.* What do you mean?

*Fred.* In my haste to do service, I never once
recollected I wanted the means. My heart was so
full, that I quite forgot my pockets were empty.

*Worth.* I cannot think, young man, you came
here to insult me,

*Fred.* Insult! Oh, my dear Sir, you do not know
me! You may soon. I have left a father, in em-
barrassments, in Russia. I have landed here, de-
pendant on an uncle's bounty; and paid my last
shilling, yesterday, to the coachman, who set me
down at his gate; but my relation is as generous as a
prince! he will, I am sure, give me a supply! and
then ——

*Worth.* And then, I would not, for worlds, draw
upon your little store. You have a superior call,
it seems, upon you; a parent in distress.

*Fred.* My father's involvements, no doubt, will
be his brother's care; and if ——

*Worth.* No more, no more! I see the workings
of your heart. Farewell! You have sensibly affected
me, and I must leave you. Repine not that your will
to do good actions outruns your power. Had the
widow been without her mite, and simply dropt a
tear for Poverty, on the moist shrine of Compassion,
it would have secured to her a page in Heaven's
register. [*Exit.*

*Fred.* Now, this is all very pretty rhodomontade;
and I'll go, directly, and argue that it is so, with my
uncle, for the good of this bluff veteran. A widow,
weeping for distress, may water the road, pleasantly
enough, for herself, to Paradise;—but if she could
shed peck-loaves, instead of tears, it would be
twenty times better for the poor's box. [*Exit.*

## ACT IV.

### SCENE I.—*A Wood, skirting a Village.*

*Enter Sir* CHARLES CROPLAND *and* OLLAPOD.

#### *Sir* CHARLES.

I'M as chilly as a bottle of Port, in a hard frost—
This is your English Spring, that our shivering
poets celebrate by a fire-side, if they can get one, and
sing of basking shepherds, making love in the sun.—
I'm as amorous as an Arcadian, but it's cursed cold,
in Kent, for all that. Are you sure these women
will come, Ollapod?

*Olla.* Sure as death, as I tell my patients.

*Sir Cha.* They find that, sure enough.

*Olla.* He! He! Yes, Sir Charles; I never de-
ceive them—Call'd in, last week, to Captain Custard, of our Corps, who was shovell'd off by a surfeit.
" Dearest friend," says I, looking in his fat face,
" be firm. — Candour compels me to say, now
" I'm come, you can't live:" he didn't — " You
" shall be buried with military honours"—he was.
Attended him from beginning to end—doctor and
mourner—Bed and grave—Physick'd him first, shot
over him afterwards. Poor fellow! a good officer,
an excellent pastry-cook, a prodigious eater, and a
profitable patient!

*Sir Cha.* Damn Captain Custard! I am thinking
of a fine girl, and you are panegyrising a dead pastry-
cook. These women will disappoint us, at last.

*Olla.* Then there's no honour in the honourable
Miss MacTab.

*Sir Cha.* You didn't see Emily?

*Olla.* No.

*Sir Cha.* Pshaw! all is uncertainty. I shall lose
the golden fruit, at last.

*Olla.* Damn'd hard, after I've given the dragon
a dose—Do you take, good Sir? do you take?

*Sir Cha.* I wish the dragon had wings, then, to move a little faster. This sharp north-easterly wind will prevent their walking.

*Olla.* I hope not, Sir Charles;—for they'll get a cursed cold, and want an apothecary. [*Aside.*

*Sir Cha.* Stay—I think I see a petticoat.

*Olla.* Mark! 'tis an old bird—The honourable Miss Mac Tab, in a jog trot.

*Sir Cha.* And Emily with her, by all that's beautiful!

*Olla.* Yes, that's she—As fine a woman as ever smelt sal volatile. There's the game, Sir Charles! You've nothing to do but to kill.

*Sir Cha.* Step aside, or our meeting will be too abrupt. We must kill by the rule here, Ollapod.

*Olla.* Kill by rule? With all my heart! 'Tis a method I've long been used to. [*They retire.*

*Enter Miss* LUCRETIA MAC TAB, *and* EMILY WORTHINGTON.

*Luc.* Cold! ridiculous! Females of fashion, Miss Emily, never complain of the cold, now.

*Emily.* I didn't know it was the fashion to be insensible, grand-aunt.

*Luc.* To the seasons it is. An English gentlewoman, of the year eighteen hundred, emulates an English oak; which is hardy as well as elegant; and beautiful, but bare, in the depth of December.

*Emily.* Dear! that's a charming park yonder! Who can it belong to?

*Luc.* Sir Charles Cropland.

*Emily.* Sir Charles Cropland! Pray, let us get home again!

*Luc.* Does a fine country frighten you, Miss Emily?

*Emily.* It used, in Canada.

*Luc.* For what reason, pray?

*Emily.* Because a brute sometimes inhabits it.

*Luc.* Ridiculous! Should we happen to meet Sir Charles, I beg that ———

*Emily.* What, is he here, then?

*Luc.* So Mr. Ollapod informs me.

*Emily.* And who is he?

*Luc.* The apothe——Hem! the officer who, visited the family, this morning.

*Emily.* We will have no more walks, without my father, madam.

*Luc.* Oh! as you please; but——Eh! I declare here they both come—'Tis impossible to avoid them now.

*Emily.* Bless me!—This is very strange!

    [Sir Charles Cropland *and* Ollapod
        *appear at the back of the scene.*

*Sir Cha.* Engage the old Tabby in talk; and move off with her, if you can.

*Olla.* Mum!—I'll bother her.

                    [*They come forward.*

*Sir Cha.* Ladies, I am rejoiced to see you. To meet you in this part of the world, is, indeed, an unexpected pleasure.

*Luc.* We are come here, you see, to rusticate, Sir Charles, as my poor dear brother, Lord Lofty, used to say.—Been vegetating here, for a week, at a wretched farm-house; but air is the grand article with me.

*Sir Cha.* At your dinner it is, I'll be sworn. [*Aside.*] And what is your grand object, in the country, Miss Worthington?

*Emily.* To be alone, Sir.

*Sir Cha.* Umph! a strange propensity, permit me to say, for one so young, and so beautiful!

*Emily.* I learned it from my father, Sir; we neither of us like intruders.

*Olla.* That's a damn'd dowse in the blubber-chops of my friend, the baronet.—I must talk to the old one—Hem! rural walks here, Ma'am—All green, and twisting, like a snake in a bottle of spirits.—Wood-pigeons in plenty.—Hear 'em cooing? Pop 'em down, here, by dozens.

        [Sir Charles *talks apart to* Emily.

*Luc.* They are pleasing birds enough, in a grove, Sir.

*Olla.* And pretty picking in a pye, Ma'am. [*Looking towards Sir* CHARLES *and* EMILY.] Yes—he's beginning — Must have Miss Mac Tab off soon. [*Aside.*] Fond of views, Ma'am? Hill, dale, steeples, rivers, tufts of trees, and the like?

*Luc.* I admire a rich landscape, Sir. When my brother, the Baron, was planting clumps round Ricketty Castle, I used to say he was placing beauty-spots on the face of nature.

*Olla.* Did you? Come, that was very well—very well, indeed! Thank you, good Madam—I owe you one. Pretty sporting country to the right. [*She turns towards Sir* CHARLES *and* EMILY. *He pulls her by the elbow.*] That's to the left Ma'am.

*Luc.* Bless me! this is a very rude man! Do you know, Sir Charles, that Emily has lost your beautiful little present?

*Sir Cha.* What, the terrier puppy, from Leicester-shire?

*Luc.* Gone—though he was in the apartment when you last did us the honour of a call.

*Sir Cha.* Unkind to set so little store by my present, Miss Worthington! and when did you observe the puppy was gone?

*Emily.* The very moment you left the room, Sir.

*Olla.* Humph! that's another dowse for the Baronet! I must get the old woman away! [*Pulls her by the elbow.*] Ma'am!

*Luc.* Lord, Sir! [*Frumpishly.*]

*Olla.* Condescend to cast your eye over that hillock—the little lump to the left there—round and black, like a bolus. From that point, you see three capital counties at once.

*Luc.* I can't say that I perceive ——

*Olla.* Stay—there's Kent—Fertile in pheasants, cherries, hops, yeomen, codlings, and cricketters— On one side Sussex — on

*Luc.* In what beauties does that abound, Sir?

*Olla.* Mutton and Dumplings.—And there's Surry —Sweet Surry!

*Luc.* For what may that be famous?

D

*Olla.* Nothing that I know of, except my cousin, Crushjaws of Carshalton, who tugs out a stump with perfect pleasure to the patient.

*[During the above,* LUCRETIA *is continually endeavouring to turn towards Sir* CHARLES *and* EMILY; *and* OLLAPOD, *constantly, prevents her.*

*Luc.* I protest I see nothing before me, but a barn.

*Olla.* That's reckon'd the only eye-sore in the view; for it totally blocks out the prospect—Fifty yards further we may see all—A little swampy here, to be sure—Better for snipe shooting. Permit me to touch the tip of your honourable little finger, and pass you over the puddles.

*Luc.* Bless me! I can never get over that stile!

*Olla.* A little gummy in the leg, I suppose. *[Aside.]* Its the easiest in England, upon the honour of a Cornet—If an ankle's exposed, I'll forfeit all the physic in my shop. This way. *[Taking her hand.]* Step out there, Ma'am. Curse 'em! the cows have been here. This way!

*[Exit, hurrying off Miss* LUCRETIA.

*Emily.* Gone! Permit me to follow my relation, Sir.

*Sir Cha.* Stay, my dear Miss Worthington; I have something of the utmost consequence to say to you.

*Emily.* Speak it quickly, then, Sir.

*Sir Cha.* Your father does not abound in riches, I take it.

*Emily.* That is of no consequence to me, Sir, if he can be happy.

*Sir Cha.* Now, I am very rich, as men of fashion go—for, my estate is not yet dipp'd above three parts of its value.

*Emily.* That can be of no consequence to me at all, Sir.

*Sir Cha.* Pardon me—for I have to propose to you—

*Emily.* What, Sir?

*Sir Cha.* Your own house in town, the run of my
estate in the country, your own chariot, two footmen,
and six hundred a-year—But you must allow me a
little time to myself—A little play at Miles's—a
little sport at Newmarket—a little hunting in Leicestershire ; and, this apart, you'll find me the most
domestic man in the world.

*Emily.* I fancy I comprehend the nature of your
jargon, Sir.

*Sir Cha.* Jargon! It is a language perfectly un-
derstood by all us young fellows in the circle of St.
James's. 'Tis the way of the world, my dear little
Simplicity !

*Emily.* Oh! how base must be the world, then,
when it makes simplicity its victim ! I have been
bred in wilds ; but the sweet breath of Nature has
inspired my soul with reason ; common to every human bosom, as the wintry blasts, that roar'd above
me, on the mountains. What does that reason tell
me, Sir?—That vice is vice, however Society may
polish it ; that seduction is still seduction, however
Fashion may sanction it ; that intellect, speaking
through simplicity, like mine, has the force of virtue to strengthen it ; while worldly sophistry must
shrink from native truth, when it proclaims, that he,
who could break a father's heart, by heaping splen-
did infamy upon his child, is a villain.——Let me
pass you, Sir !

*Enter* FREDERICK *at the back of the scene.*

*Fred.* I have lost my way, and my uncle, and—
eh ! who have we here?

*Sir Cha.* [*Detaining* EMILY.] Upon my soul, you
must not go.

*Emily.* How, Sir?

*Sir Cha.* Look ye, my dear Emily—I am ad-
vanced too far in the game to recede. If you are not
mine by entreaty, there are four spanking greys,
ready harness'd in Cropland Park, here, that shall
whisk us to town in a minute.

*Emily.* You dare not, sure ——

*Sir Cha.* Nay, faith, I dare any thing now—for

the prize is in my reach, and I will clasp it, though your heart were colder to me than the snows of Russia. [*He runs towards her, she screams*—FRE-DERICK *advances*.]

*Fred.* [*Standing between Sir* CHARLES *and* EMI-LY.] I bring news from that country, Sir—I arrived last night.

*Sir Cha.* Then, Sir, you arrived damn'd *mal à propos.* What are you?

*Fred.* A man—so, I am bound to protect females from brutality. You, it seems, assault them. Pray, Sir, what are *you?*

*Sir Cha.* A person of some figure here, Sir. You may not know, perhaps, the consequence of insulting one of that description in this country.

*Fred.* Faith, not I: but I know the consequence of his persisting to persecute a woman in my presence.

*Sir Cha.* What may that be?

*Fred.* I knock him down.

*Sir Cha.* You will please to recollect, Sir, I am a gentleman.

*Fred.* I can't for the soul of me—I can never recollect that any man is a gentleman, when I find him forgetting it himself.

*Sir Cha.* Can you fight, Sir?

*Fred.*—Like a game cock, Sir—try me.

*Sir Cha.* What is your weapon, Sir?

*Fred.* The Knout.

*Sir Cha.* What the devil's that?

*Fred.* A Russian cat o'nine tails, to chastise a criminal; and I know no criminal who more richly deserves it than he who degrades manhood, by offering violence to the amiable sex, which nature form'd him to defend. Fear nothing, Madam.

*Sir Cha.* We must meet again, my hot spark.

*Fred.* I'm happy to hear it—It implies you are going now.

*Sir Cha.* Hark ye, Sir—I am call'd Sir Charles Cropland. Yonder is my park.

*Fred.* With four spanking greys in it. I heard you say so.

*Sir Cha.* There is very retired shooting in some parts of it, Sir—Your name.

*Fred.* Frederick Bramble;—nephew to your neighbour, Sir Robert. You'll find me ready to take a morning's sport with you.

*Sir Cha.* You shall hear from me. This is a cursed business!—but it will keep up the noise of my name at the Clubs; and the duel of a dashing Baronet furnishes food for the newspapers. [*Exit.*

*Fred.* Victory, Madam. The enemy is fled, and virtue triumphs in the field. Ha! you look pale!

*Emily.* I have been sadly flurried. [*Much agitated*]

*Fred.* 'Sdeath! she is near fainting!—Let me support you, Madam. [*She appears sinking, he catches her.*] Zounds! how beautiful she is! Tears; now would I give the world to kiss them off, and then kick the scoundrel that caused them.

*Emily.* [*Recovering.*] I know not how to thank you, Sir.

*Fred.* I'm glad of it, Ma'am—I never like to be thank'd for merely doing my duty.

*Emily.* I fear, Sir, that—I mean, I hope that—I—I hope, Sir, you will not be exposed to further danger, on my account.

*Fred.* I am not used to think of danger, Madam, on any account; but, something tells me, I shou'd glory in any that I risk'd for you. Whither shall I have the honour of attending you safe home, Madam?

*Emily.* I have a relation, Sir—a female relation, who has been walking with me: she is now, I fancy, in the next field, and she will——

*Fred.* What, an elderly lady, that I observed just now, as I pass'd, with an officer?

*Emily.* Aye—that officer!

*Fred.* Who is he, pray?

*Emily.* A wicked accessary, I am convinced, of Sir Charles Cropland's!

*Fred.* Is he? I see him coming—huzza! I'll blow him to the devil, if he were generalissimo.

*Emily.* For heaven's sake! you make me tremble.

*Fred.* Tremble! I wouldn't give *you* pain for worlds! I'll be calm with him—On your account I will. I'll affront him with all the civility imaginable.

*Enter* OLLAPOD, *hastily.*

*Olla.* The honourable Miss Mac Tab has tumbled up to her middle in the mud. Bless me, is Sir Charles gone?

*Fred.* You are Sir Charles's friend, it seems, Sir?

*Olla.* I have the honour to be close in his confidence.

*Fred.* And assist him upon honourable occasions. You are an officer, I perceive.

*Olla.* He! he! yes, Sir—Cornet in our volunteer Corps of Cavalry; as respectable a body as any regulars in christendom.

*Fred.* I don't doubt it all. To stand forward at home, and keep off invaders from the shores of our country, is as honourable, and praise-worthy, as marching to attack its enemies abroad. Pray, don't be alarm'd—you see I'm civil. [*Aside to* EMILY.]

*Olla.* A pretty spoken young man—I'll encourage him. Come, that's very well—very well indeed! Thank you, good Sir—I owe you one.

*Fred.* But some morbid parts may be found, I fancy, in the wholesomest bodies.

*Olla.* Decidedly.—Like a chubby child, in high health, with a whitlow.

*Fred.* Just such a whitlow I take you to be.

*Olla.* Me!

*Fred.* Exactly: and 'tis that uniform alone—as I respect every symbol of loyalty and patriotism,—that prevents my cropping your ears as close as your jacket. Don't be uneasy, you see I'm civil.

[*To* EMILY.

*Olla.* Crop! Zounds! what do you mean?

*Fred.* Can't you take my meaning, in your own way?

*Olla.* Way! Sir, I engage to kill the enemies of my country, in the way of war,—I never draw blood from the natives, but in the way of business.

*Fred.* Business!

*Olla.* Yes; I'm an apothecary—Take care how you meddle with a man of my repute. Served my time seven years, under old Cataplasm, of Canterbury;—took out my freedom in that ancient city;—thumpt the mortar, six months, at Maidstone;—now, on my own bottom, in trade, at Tunbridge. Cornet Ollapod, at the gilt Galen's-head; known to all the nobility round—Sharp shot in a copse—deep dab at the broad sword exercise—Charge a furze-bush, wing a wood-cock, or blister a Lord, with any chap in the county. Insult me as an officer, and I'll prosecute you—Touch my ears, you touch my honour, and damn me, I'll clap you in the county jail, for assaulting a freeman. [*Exit.*

*Fred.* That scarlet apothecary is beneath my notice: but if the fellow has flurried your nerves, Madam, which it is his trade to tranquillize, I'll pound him to death, in his own mortar.

*Emily.* Pray, do not be so violent:—It terrifies me—On your own account, Sir, it terrifies me.

*Fred.* On my own account?

*Emily.* Yes. It would grieve me to see one, who is capable of such kind actions towards me, hurried into peril, by the warmth of his temper.

*Fred.* I will be what you please. Tell me only whither I shall lead you. You are of the neighbourhood, I conjecture. May I ask your name?

*Emily.* Emily Worthington, Sir.

*Fred.* Worthington! then you are daughter to the finest spirited man I ever met in my life.

*Emily.* Do you think so? Do you, indeed? I am very glad that you think so. But how came you acquainted?

*Fred.* Why, I —— I had a little business with him;—but, somehow or other, I —— I went without my credentials. Shall I take you to him? Will you trust yourself with me?

*Emily.* Trust myself! Oh yes! My dear father shall thank you. I will thank you; and our poor old Corporal, who has served in the wars, and fol-

low'd us through America, he will thank you, in
tears of joy, when he hears of this rescue.

*Fred.* That old Corporal loves you then?

*Emily.* Certainly he does.   He nursed me when
my poor mother died, and left me an infant in Gibraltar; and dearly I love him, too.

*Fred.* Now, what would I give to be an old Corporal! [*Aside.*] I attend you.—Let me see you home.
Oh! how would it diminish the number of scoun-
drels in the world, if they could once taste the joys
of rescuing a lovely female from perdition, and re-
storing her to her father!             [*Exeunt.*

SCENE II.—*Before* HARROWBY'S *house.*

*Enter* WORTHINGTON, *from the house.*

*Worth.* Emily not yet returned!—I cannot rest in
this suspence—Every instant, I dread the arrival of
these officers to drag me from my family, from my
child!—Ha! two strangers lurking yonder! Nay,
then, I know their errand—Where is my Emily?
Well, well, 'tis better, in such a struggle, if the
child witness not the anguish of the parent.   [*Goes
up the stage.*]

*Enter Sir* ROBERT BRAMBLE, *and* HUMPHREY
DOBBINS.

*Sir Rob.* So: here we are at last—That hill's a
breather.   I am sure that was my nephew I saw
hopping over the plough'd land, yonder.

*Dob.* Not a morsel like him.

*Sir Rob.* I wonder if the rogue has found his way
here yet.—Ha!—There's our man, — leaning against
the stump of the tree, there.   He seems lost in
thought—Go, and tap him on the shoulder, Humphrey.

*Dob.* [*Putting his hand on* WORTHINGTON's
shoulder.] You're wanted.

*Worth.* [*Coming forward.*]   I understand you.

*Sir Rob.* Your servant, Sir—Your name is Worthington, they tell me.

*Worth.* It is, friend.

*Sir Rob.* I have a little business with you; and it is'nt my way to use ceremony.

*Worth.* I expect none, from a person of your stamp.

*Sir Rob.* Stamp!—Humphrey, is'nt that odd?

*Dob.* Not a bit—The neighbours tell every body what a rum jockey you are.

*Sir Rob.* Umph! you'll excuse me for talking before old Crabbed here—He's in all my affairs—The puppy has grown grey with me, and I can't well do without him.

*Worth.* Your follower, I suppose.

*Sir Rob.* Yes, he's always at my heels. You have served his Majesty, I hear, and done your duty nobly.

*Worth.* No matter—Do your duty, and 'tis enough.

*Sir Rob.* Yes, he's as proud as lucifer, I see—but there's no flattery in that. [*Aside.*] The motives that brought me here, will prove, I trust, that I don't always neglect my duty.

*Worth.* You may perform it now, then—If my life depended on it, friend, I could not give you five pounds, at this moment.

*Sir Rob.* Give me five pounds! Who the devil wishes you? I want to know how I can do you a kindness.

*Worth.* I thank you.—In consideration, then, for a gentleman, and in reliance on his honour to acknowledge the obligation, when in his power, I trust you will place me in an apartment in your own house.

*Sir Rob.* An apartment in my own house!

*Worth.* Yes—where I may have the comfort of privacy, and my family about me.

*Sir Rob.* Damn me, but that is pretty plump, for a man who would sooner see me hang'd than ask me a favour! [*Aside.*]

*Worth.* You will not, I think, be harsh enough to lodge me among the wretched rabble, who are the common inmates of your gloomy walls.

*Sir Rob.* My gloomy walls! an infernal, impudent old scoundrel! Squeezes himself, and all his relations, into my house, and calls my family a wretched rabble. [*Aside.*] Humphrey, did you ever see such brass?

*Dob.* I always told you, except myself, you kept but a queer set.

*Sir Rob.* Zounds, I'll——No, I'll keep my temper. Pray, Sir, what can you suppose I am to make of your?

*Worth.* Make of me! —These mercenary harpies! I have already told you, friend, you can make nothing of me, in my present situation—What you think you may make of me, in future, as a man of honour, I leave to your own feelings.

*Sir Rob.* I won't consult my own feelings now, Sir; I must proceed upon my judgment.

*Worth.* I know you are proceeding upon a judgment.

*Sir Rob.* And that judgment is cursedly against you, at this moment, let me tell you.

*Worth.* 'Tis my misfortune.

*Sir Rob.* If you think that a misfortune, you might as well alter your conduct with me a little, I don't see the drift on't.

*Worth.* Drift!

*Sir Rob.* Aye; where's the policy?

*Worth.* That expired but a few hours too soon.

*Sir Rob.* His policy expired but a few hours too soon! Why, the man's a maniac! His distresses have deranged him. Were you—hem—were you ever wounded in the head?

*Worth.* Truce with interrogations, friend. I am ready to accompany you.

*Sir Rob.* You are! And, pray, where are we to go?

*Worth.* I told you I should give your own house the preference.

*Sir Rob.* Curse me if you ever set your foot over my threshold!

*Worth.* Lead me where you please, then. You

proferr'd kindness, and I was weak enough to expect
it. But I might have known that one of your cast
is deaf to the petition of distress.

*Sir Rob.* The devil I am!

*Worth.* Familiar with scenes of want, habit har-
dens your heart, till the very face becomes an index
of the mind; and callous inhumanity scowls in every
lineament of the hard-featured bailiff.

*Sir Rob.* Blood and thunder! Bailiff! Humphrey,
do I look a bit like a bailiff?

*Dob.* I don't know but you do.

*Sir Rob.* Sir—I—pardon your mistake, and I like
your spirit—There's no flattery in it. But I'm in a
passion for all that. Many a modern Sir Jacky looks
like a prize-fighter; but its rather hard to take a
Baronet of the old school for a bum-bailiff.

*Worth.* My daughter!

*Sir Rob.* And my sky-rocket of a nephew.

*Enter* FREDERICK *and* EMILY.

*Fred.* Ha! you are here at last, I perceive, uncle.

*Worth.* Uncle! Is this Sir Robert Bramble,
then? the generous relation, of whom you told me?

*Sir Rob.* Generous! Psha! But I am his uncle;
—though the puppy's smart enough, he is nephew
to the hard-featured fellow, whose face is an index
of his mind.

*Emily.* Oh, Sir, if you are his relation, talk to
him, I entreat you—argue with him——

*Sir Rob.* Argue with him! that I will, with all
my heart and soul! On what subject?

*Emily.* On his rash intention, Sir, to meet the
ruffian from whom he has just rescued me.

*Worth.* Rescued you, Emily! What does this
mean?

*Fred.* Oh—a mere trifle—nothing—A gentleman,
in the fields, here, happen'd to be so very civil to
Miss Worthington, that I took it for rudeness—so
I happen'd to be so rude to him, that he could'nt
take it for civility, that's all.

*Worth.* Rudeness to my child! Who has dared to
—But, come in, Emily—Your pardon, Sir. [*To Sir*

Robert.]  You have found nothing but confusion
here, and I must retire with my daughter, for an explanation.  Come, Emily.

*Emily.* Let us thank this gentleman, before we
go, Sir.

*Fred.* Upon my soul, I deserve no thanks, Sir.
If I deserve opinion more——

*Emily.* [*To* Fred.] Farewell, Sir!—And, pray,
pray be cautious.

               [*Exeunt* Worthington *and* Emily.

*Sir Rob.* Frederick, who is the fellow you have
been quarrelling with?

*Fred.* He calls himself Sir Charles Cropland.

*Sir Rob.* I know him—He's a puppy—must you
fight him?

*Fred.* So he tells me.

*Sir Rob.* I'll be your second.

*Fred.* You!

*Sir Rob.* Yes—; fighting's a sort of sharp argument; and, as we defend the cause of insulted inno-
cence, it's damn'd hard if we hav'nt the best on't.
But hark ye, you dog—don't fall in love with the
girl.

*Fred.* I have——

*Sir Rob.* You hav'n't!

*Fred.* Over head and ears.

*Sir Rob.* Why, you blockhead, she's a beggar.

*Fred.* So am I—We shall make a very pretty
couple.

*Sir Rob.* And, if you married, how would you
support her?

*Fred.* Perhaps, you would support us.

*Sir Rob.* You sha'n't have a shilling, till my death.

*Fred.* Then I hope we shall have the pleasure of
starving together, a great while, Sir.

*Sir Rob.* Run back, and order a dinner for a party.
Tell Old Buncles, the butler, to lug out some claret.

*Fred.* Then after dinner, I'll drink Emily Worthington in a pint bumper.          [*Exit.*

*Sir Rob.* Humphrey, you haven't attended, now,
to a word of what was passing.

*Dob.* Every syllable on't.

*Sir Rob.* You'll laugh to see me out in a duel, I suppose.

*Dob.* No, I sha'n't—I'd sooner be shot at myself.

*Sir Rob.* Umph! If my nephew marries this girl! I've a great mind to cut him off with a shilling.

*Dob.* No you won't.

*Sir Rob.* Why, you know he's as poor as a rat.

*Dob.* The rat's your relation—It wou'd be plaguy hard to starve him, when you feed all the rest of the rats in the parish.

*Sir Rob.* Come along, Humphrey—And if ever you starve, rank bacon, and mouldy pye-crust, be my portion!　　　　　　　　　　　[*Exeunt.*

## ACT V.

### SCENE I.—*A Wood, and a Path Way.*

#### Enter OLLAPOD.

AN awkward errand I'm on, to Sir Robert Bramble's. Not quite correct to carry a challenge into a family I have physick'd. But honour, in this case, before medicine: a leaf of laurel's worth twenty drops of laudanum. Mars is first customer, and damn Æsculapius! Ha! here comes the enemy, cp hid, from the house! The game meets me half way, as Death does the Doctor.　　　　[*Steps aside.*

#### Enter FREDERICK.

*Fred.* "A pointed pain pierced deep my heart,"
　　"A swift cold trembling seized on every part."

*Olla.* That's an ague.

*Fred.* "But quickly to my cost I found,"
　　"'Twas Love, not Death, had made the wound."

*Olla.* Damn that disease! it's cured without an apothecary.

*Fred.* I've order'd dinner for my old uncle; and now, can't I, for my life, help loitering about the farm-house. What mind she has in ev'ry look! I would rather be a whale, and flounce about the Baltick, than fall in love with a fine proportion'd face of beautiful insipidity — 'Tis a lamp without oil— Heaven in a fog——Give me those dear bewitching features, where sweet expression always speaks, and sometimes sparkles. Give me a dimpled beauty that —— Zounds! here's that damn'd ugly apothecary! Pray, Sir, do you know what are some men's antipathies?

*Olla.* Yes; cats, rats, old maids, double-tripe, spiders, Cheshire cheese, and cork-cutters.

*Fred.* Now, my antipathy, Sir, is a pert apothecary. How dare you look me again in the face, without trembling?

*Olla.* Trembling at what?

*Fred.* Death!

*Olla.* Pooh! I've made it my business to look Death in the face for fifteen years, and don't tremble at it at all.

*Fred.* Why do you presume, Sir, to come across me here?

*Olla.* Here! this is the King's highway—trod on as common as camomile—crowded with all comers, like the Red Cow on a field day. Besides, I've business at Blackberry Hall.

*Fred.* At my uncle's?

*Olla.* Yes; I've something in my pocket to deliver there. You may guess what it is.

*Fred.* Lip-salve for the maid, perhaps; or rose-water to put into puddings.

*Olla.* Damn lips, and puddings! I've a letter for you.

*Fred.* You have!

*Olla.* Yes; to be taken directly. [*Gives it.*] Eh! isn't that Sir Robert Bramble?

*Enter Sir* ROBERT BRAMBLE.

*Sir Rob.* I've sprain'd my back, trying to frisk over that infernal farmer's hog trough. If Humphrey hadn't argued I was too stiff in the joints to jump, I'd have seen the dog at the devil before I attempted

it. Ha—Mr. Ollapod—Your servant—Your servant—Tell me what brings you this way?

*Olla.* I'll see you in a fever first. [*Aside.*] Dry
weather for walking, Sir Robert—but no news—
young partridges look'd for every day—so are six
Hamburgh mails—Glad to find our gout is gone, Sir
Robert—Happy to meet you again on a good foot-
ing. Do you take, good Sir? do you take?

*Sir Rob.* I take your Jokes, as I do your bottles
of physick, Master Ollapod.

*Olla.* How is that, Sir Robert?

*Sir Rob.* I never take them at all.

*Olla.* Come, that's very well; very well, indeed!
Thank you, good Sir—I owe you one.

*Sir Rob.* [*Seeing* FREDERICK.] Frederick! what
are you doing here?

*Fred.* Reading a challenge, uncle.

*Sir Rob.* So!—'tis come then.—Who brought it?

*Fred.* Pestle and mortar there. Read, uncle,
read!

*Sir Rob.* [*Reading.*]

    " Sir,

" Mr. Ollapod, of the Volunteer Corps, will de-
" liver this to you. You will find me, half an hour
" hence, at the plantation on the heath, waiting to
" receive the satisfaction due to

                " Your humble servant,
                    " CHARLES CROPLAND."

Plain as a demonstration in Euclid.—[*Turns to*
OLLAPOD.] But how dare you, who have bled my
coachman, till he can't drive, and julep'd my cook,
till she faints at a fire, administer a challenge to my
nephew?.....

*Olla.* Honour is rigid, Sir Robert, and must be
minded as strictly as a milk diet.

*Sir Rob.* You come here, in short, as Sir Charles
Cropland's friend?

*Olla.* I do. Gallipots must give way to gallant
feelings—and Galen is gagg'd by Bellona. Sorry
to offend the Bramble Family. Shall bring lint,

probe, and styptick, along with the pistols. Though
serving as second, on one side, shall be proud to
extract a ball for either party, on as reasonable terms
as any in the profession.                    [*Exit.*

*Fred.* I have been thinking, uncle, and——you
sha'n't accompany me in this business.

*Sir Rob.* I sha'n't! You puppy, hav'n't I a right
to smell powder, if I please?

*Fred.* Tis an awkward business, altogether,—perhaps a foolish one.   I am a useless fellow, floating
through the world like a mere feather.   If I am
blown out of sight, 'tis no matter.   You are of too
much value, uncle, to be made the sport of every
idle gale.

*Sir Rob.* Now, what, in the devil's name, is the
value of man, if he don't stand by his friend, when
he wants him?

*Fred.* And what, in the devil's name, uncle, is
the value of his friend, if he only drags him into a
scrape?

*Sir Rob.* A scrape!

*Fred.* Yes.—They tell me the law of this country
is apt to call killing a man, in a duel, murder; and
to look on all accessaries as principals.   Now, uncle,
as I am going on an expedition which may end in
hanging, I don't think it quite considerate to invei-
gle an honest friend to be of the party.

*Sir Rob.* I never heard 'the argument put in
that way before.   There are few, I fancy, of your
opinion.

*Fred.* Oh, a great many.   There are men enough
to be found, who would give in the same opinion,
by Twelve at a time.   But should I fall, in my encounter with this booby of a Baronet ——

*Sir Rob.* Fall!

*Fred.* Why, 'twould be bold to argue, uncle, if
a bullet hits in a mortal place, that it won't kill—
and in case of the worst, I have a request to make—

*Sir Rob.* [*Uneasy.*]   Well?

*Fred.* If I fall, then, uncle, you—You know I
have a father.

*Sir Rob.* [*Agitated.*] Well!

*Fred.* He is your brother, my dear unc¹! An affectionate brother. Your tempers may not assimilate, but he loves you.—He is poor. [*Takes him by the hand.*]—If I fall, remember him.

*Sir Rob.* [*Throws himself on* FREDERICK'S *neck.*] My dear, dear Frederick! your death would break my heart—I have been reasoning all my life, and find that all argument will vanish before one touch of nature.

*Fred.* I fancy you will often find it so, my dear uncle.

*Sir Rob.* And nature tells me, if you argue for ages, you sha'n't prevent the old man's going with you. Come, we must go home to prepare—You must have my pistols, and—upon my soul, Frederick, I love my brother Job—We'll have him over, and — zounds! this will all end in smoke—and then I'll write to Russia—We'll have a family party, and be jolly, and —Come, my dear lad, come!            [*Exeunt.*

SCENE II —*The Parlour in* HARROWBY'S *House.*

*Enter* WORTHINGTON.

*Worth.* This young man may rashly plunge into a quarrel on Emily's account. 'Tis *my* duty to chastise the insulter of my child. At Sir Robert Bramble's I might learn more, and——but, in what a state of mind should I attend him!

*Enter* Corporal FOSS.

So, Corporal! have you observed any people about the house.

*Foss.* No enemies, your honour; unless they are in ambuscade.

*Worth.* I am strongly inclined to go to Sir Robert's to day.

*Foss.* I hope your honour will. They say he is such a good-hearted old gentleman—Ten to one but he gives your honour a helping hand.

*Worth.* Then he'll think I come to solicit assistance! I will not go. [*Half aside.*]

*Foss.* Won't you, your honour?

E

*Worth.* I wish to see my daughter again, Corporal.

*Foss.* I had almost made sure of your honour's going—I have laid out the red roquelaure; and, in case of a dark night, Stephen's now in the stable, dusting out the lantern, for me, to march home before your honour.

*Worth.* Well, well,—send Emily to the ——

*Foss.* Heigho! Oh, here comes my young lady!

Enter EMILY.

[*Aside to* EMILY.] Make him go to Sir Robert's, Miss Emily—Bless you, do!—Mollify his honour a bit—You don't know half the good may come on't —Do now!                    [*Exit Foss.*

*Worth.* What said the Corporal, Emily?

*Emily.* He bid me press our going to Sir Robert Bramble's to-day.

*Worth.* Should you wish me, Emily, to place myself in a situation where I might be suspected of imploring support?

*Emily.* Heaven forbid! But the gentleman, who protected me, has been so good, —so *very* good,—that ————

*Worth.* That what, Emily?

*Emily.* I——should like to thank him——that's all.

*Worth.* Have we not both thanked him, already?

*Emily.* Yes—but—not enough, perhaps.

*Worth.* If more be necessary, I may express our further sense of his goodness by letter.

*Emily.* The service he did me was not by letter, you know, my dear father.

*Worth.* You seem strangely interested here, Emily!

*Emily.* Shouldn't I be so! I hope I ought: for indeed, indeed—I—I am very uneasy. [*Unable to suppress her tears.*]

*Worth.* My child!—uneasy!—compose yourself, Emily.—Open your heart to me; to your father; your friend, Emily!

*Emily.* Indeed, I never wish to hide my thoughts

from you. They often meet your ear so wild, and so unform'd, that they resemble dreams.

*Worth.* Alas, my child! the thoughts of young minds too frequently resemble dreams;—dawning dreams of happiness, my Emily, which vanish as our day opens. Should you love this young man, Emily, it is a dream from which no reproof of mine shall startle you; but the gentleness of a father shall awaken you.

*Emily.* Love him! Oh, no:—but, he preserved me from danger, and, on that account, I dread he may incur it himself.

*Worth.* You know not, yet, what your heart is, Emily.

*Emily.* Yes, indeed, I do.—I should be grieved if I did not know it dearly loved you.

*Worth.* And you have no such sentiments towards this young man, Emily?

*Emily.* No, upon my word. The sentiments I feel for him are as different as light and darkness.

*Worth.* My dearest Emily, till you know the world's path better, be cautious how you tread. Lovely blossoms open ere the fruit is form'd, and the heart expands before the judgment ripens, I may soon be snatch'd from you, Emily ———

*Emily.* My father!

*Worth.* Disappointment, too, may press on the heel of age, and hasten his step with me to the grave.

*Emily.* My dearest father!

*Worth.* Take, then, my fondest counsel while I live—my best legacy, alas! should I be hurried from you. Act not too suddenly on ideas. Doubt that passion may mislead you, till reflection justifies your impulse. Wed not for wealth, Emily, without love; 'tis gaudy slavery;—nor for love without competence; 'tis twofold misery. Go not against the current of your station nor deserts. — Glide gently down the stream, with neither too-full a sail, nor too slight a freightage, and may your voyage, my child, be happier—much happier than your father's!

*Enter* Foss.

*Foss.* Madam MacTab wants to know if you all
dine at Sir Robert's, your honour ?

*Worth.* Why does she inquire, Corporal ?

*Foss.* It's about putting on some of her trinkums,
and furbelows, I fancy, your honour. She came in
a while ago, as muddy as our little pidgeon-toed
drummer, after a long march.

*Worth.* I have thought on't—Tell her we shall go.

*Foss.* No ! Will you ? Huzza ! I ha'n't been better pleased since they made me a Corporal.   [*Exit.*

*Emily.* You will go, then ?

*Worth.* Some explanation is necessary there, and
I will make up my mind to bury other feelings.   I
might hesitate, perhaps, in taking you with me, but
you have heard my counsel, and I know my child.
Lucretia will go with us—We must, afterwards, take
our leave of her entirely.

*Emily.* Indeed !

*Worth.* Her conduct, of which you have inform'd
me, with Sir Charles Cropland, has decided me; and
she will only quit a tottering asylum.   I have to tell
you our friend Burford is dead, Emily.

*Emily.* What ! the friend that——

*Worth.* Yes, Emily—A worthy, an honourable
man—but from the suddenness of his death——'tis
fit I prepare you for the shock—he has left me in
involvements, which, in a few hours, may enclose
me in a prison.

*Emily.* A prison ! You !—You will take me with
you—Won't you take me with you ?

*Worth.* Like the eagle on the rock, Emily, I
must shelter my nestling where Providence ordains.

*Emily.* Well, then, do not make yourself unhappy, my dear father ! We shall not be very miserable, if we are not asunder.—I will sit by you—
talk to you—listen to you—and, should a tear steal
upon your cheek, I can kiss it off,—and [*Sobs invo-
luntarily*]—I am not shock'd for myself—pray, forgive me !

*Worth.* My beloved, my amiable child !

*Enter Miss* LUCRETIA MAC TAB.

*Luc.* If we live here for a twelvemonth, I'll never speak to that beastly quack, who left me in a ditch, again.

*Worth.* We shall not live here for a twelvemonth, Madam; and, after what has pass'd, you will feel as little surprise, as I mean offence, when I propose to you to relinquish the fortunes of a man, whose situation, in all places, must be so irksome to you.

*Luc.* I——I understand—You are weak enough then, Mr. Worthington, to wish me to withdraw my countenance from the family.

*Worth.* Since the strength of your zeal for my family, Madam, has so far outrun my weak notions of its happiness, I confess I do wish you to withdraw it!

*Luc.* 'Tis very well, Sir!

*Worth.* When you are ready, Madam, to go to Sir Robert Bramble's, you will find Emily, and me, in the garden, prepared to attend you. Come, my love! *[Exeunt* EMILY *and* WORTHINGTON.

*Luc.* Then the honourable Miss Lucretia Mac Tab is cut, at last, by a half-pay lieutenant, in a marching regiment.

*Enter* FOSS.

*Foss.* Is your ladyship's honour ready to go?

*Luc.* Go! Are you sent to drum me out, fellow, as you would a deserter?

*Foss.* I don't come to drum your ladyship's honour;—I want to know if you'll go to Sir Robert's?

*Luc.* Go, to-morrow, by break of day, to the post-house. Ask if there's a return chaise there, for London.

*Foss.* What am I to do then, an' it please you?

*Luc.* Secure a seat in it, for the Honourable Miss Lucretia MacTab.

*Foss.* Is your ladyship's honour bundling off, then?

*Luc.* Bundling, you brute! obey my orders.

*Foss.* That I will, with all my heart and soul, an' please your honour!

*Luc.* I'll withdraw myself from this wretched family—I'll go down to Scotland, and patronise my
sixteenth cousin, the tobacconist of Glasgow. [*Exit.*

*Enter* STEPHEN.

*Stephen.* Here be the lantern, Master Corporal.
I have made him shine like our barn door. If you
do like a duck, now, for your supper, I ha' shot one
of ourn for you, wi' father's blunderbuss.

*Foss.* How came you to do that, my honest lad?

*Stephen.* Why, she ware a marching before a
whole brood of young ones—and look'd, for all the
world, like a captain at the head of his attachment.
We have no herbs to stuff her, for I ha' cut up all
our kitchen garden, to look like a mortification.

*Foss.* Well, well—I must attend his honour—But
keep a sharp look-out, my good lad!—You know
what I told you.

*Stephen.* What, about the bum-baileys? rotum!
I'll blow 'em up wi' gunpowder.

*Foss.* Keep a good watch, that's all.

*Stephen.* Dang me, if a soldier's hurt on our pre-
mises. I've unmuzzled Towzer and Cabbage; they'll
bite all as come, good or bad. Come you along,
Mr. Corporal. " For a Soldier, a soldier's the lad
" for me!" [*Singing.*] [*Exeunt.*

SCENE *the last.*

*Enter* Sir CHARLES CROPLAND *and* OLLAPOD.

*Sir Cha.* We are on the ground first.

*Olla.* Perhaps the enemy's subject to a common
complaint.

*Sir Cha.* What's that?

*Olla.* Troubled with a palpitation of heart, and
can't come.

*Sir Cha.* He doesn't seem of that sort. What are
the odds now, that he doesn't wing me? These
greenhorns generally hit every thing but the man
they aim at.

*Olla.* Do they! zounds! then the odds are that
he'll wing me—I'll be principal, if you please;—

for, to say the truth, I never served my time to the trade of a second.

*Sir Cha.* Psha! You must measure the distance, when he comes, Ollapod.

*Olla.* What's the usual distance, Sir Charles?

*Sir Cha.* Eight paces.

*Olla.* Bless me! men might as well fight across a counter. Does the second always measure the ground?

*Sir Cha.* 'Tis the custom.

*Olla.* Then you had better have chosen one a little longer in the legs. If I was to fight, I'd come out with a Colossus.

*Sir Cha.* I see him coming to the style.

*Olla.* There! he has jump'd over. Curse him! he's as nimble as quicksilver—And there's old Sir Robert, waddling behind him, like a badger.

*Sir Cha.* They are here.

*Enter Sir* ROBERT BRAMBLE *and* FREDERICK.

*Sir Rob.* Gently, Frederick! I tell you I'm out of breath.

*Fred.* We shall be too late, and——Oh! here's my man. I hope we hav'n't kept you waiting, Sir. They say, in England, when people are to shoot at one another, it's the only engagement in which it's the fashion to be punctual.

*Sir Cha.* You are pretty exact, Sir.

*Fred.* Let us lose no time, if you please, then;—for dinner will be spoil'd.

*Sir Cha.* Perhaps, Sir, one of us may never go to dinner again.

*Fred.* No; but my uncle will—and 'twould be pity he should have his meat over-roasted.

*Sir Cha.* Mr. Ollapod, be so good as to walk over the ground.

*Olla.* Left foot foremost, as they do in the Infantry?

*Sir Rob.* Hold, Sir Charles! Perhaps this matter may be brought to an accommodation.

*Sir Cha.* I don't well see how, Sir Robert.

*Sir Rob.* If you are alive to fair argument, I think I shall convince you you have been cursedly in the wrong.

*Sir Cha.* I didn't come here to argue, Sir.

*Sir Rob.* Didn't you! Frederick, you must shoot him. A man that won't listen to argument deserves to be blown to the devil.

*Olla.* [*Finishing his measurement.*] Five, six, seven, eight.

*Fred.* We'll take our ground if you please, Sir.

*Sir Cha.* Give me that, Ollapod; and success to hair-triggers! [*Takes a pistol from* OLLAPOD.]

*Sir Rob.* Here is your pistol, my dear lad.— Zounds! my heart is as heavy as a bullet! Happen what will, I shall never forget poor Job; and as for you, Frederick—Come, damn it, we mustn't blubber now. [*They take their ground, and present.*]

*Olla.* Stop—here's somebody coming—Medical men never witness'd a finer crisis!

### Enter WORTHINGTON.

*Worth.* My friend! Sir Robert Bramble, too! pistols!

*Fred.* Stand out of the way, my dear Sir! Whoever is on his legs, after the first fire, will have the pleasure of speaking to you.

*Worth.* Stay, gentlemen! This business, I believe, requires my interference.

*Sir Cha.* And pray, Sir, what may make your interference so necessary?

*Worth.* I conceive you to be Sir Charles Cropland;—which argues———

*Sir Rob.* Don't waste your arguments: they'll be all thrown away upon him.

*Sir Cha.* I am Sir Charles Cropland, Sir; and, pray, who are you?

*Worth.* I will tell you, Sir.—I am a man, into whose family a serpent has basely crept, to corrupt my child; but her mind is fraught with too much sense and virtue, to fall beneath his wiles; and, ruffian-like, he has attempted force to complete his purposes. I am an officer, Sir, in his Majesty's army—quick to resent a private injury, as I have been ready to face my country's foes. I am one, Sir, who am as gratified to meet you, that I may chastise you, as you merit,—as you have ever been industrious to skulk from me, conscious of the punishment you have deserved. I need not tell you my name is Worthington.

*Sir Rob.* Dam'me, but that is better than argument; and as unlike flattery as any thing I ever heard in my life !

*Fred.* [*To Sir* CHARLES.] Now, pray, Sir, are you and I to go home to our dinners, or are we to swallow a forced-meat ball in the fields?

*Sir Cha.* We had better suspend the business, Sir —There are ladies coming.

### *Enter* LUCRETIA *and* EMILY.

*Luc.* Your father has trotted on, child, as if he was on a forced march. Bless me ! [*Looking round*] who have we here ?

*Emily.* My father—with Sir Robert, and——ha! Sir Charles Cropland there !

*Luc.* And that brute who left me in the mire.

*Olla.* That's me.

*Worth.* You and I, Sir Charles, must find another moment for explanation.

*Sir Cha.* The immediate moment may be the best, Mr. Worthington. I believe I may have been so fashionable in my ideas, that they may have led me wrong; and I don't think it a very bad style, though it mayn't be modern, to confess it.

*Worth.* The style of sense and honesty, Sir, must ever meet approbation; that of folly, contempt; that of offence, correction; and, I should be sorry if the style of repentance did not find forgiveness.

*Sir Rob.* Or the style of argument, listeners.

*Sir Cha.* Miss Worthington, I confess my fault, and plead for pardon. You will not only, I hope, afford me your own, but intercede with Mr. Wor-

thington for his, also. You check'd me—[*To* Fred.]
rather roughly indeed—in a career which I have ac-
knowledged to be wrong, Sir.—Instead, therefore,
of proceeding in resentment, it will be better to
offer you my thanks, if you will be pleased to accept
them.

*Fred.* Sir, 'tis pleasanter to be thank'd than shot
at any time; and I accept them willingly.

*Sir Cha.* I take my leave then. I hav'n't dash'd
thro' this scrape according to present principles—
a man's owning he is sorry for his vices may get him
laugh'd at, among a few gay friends, who have more
spirits than thought; but I believe he'll hunt the
pleasanter for it, in Leicestershire. [*Exit.*

*Olla.* [*Advancing.*] Miss Lucretia Mac Tab, I
confess my fault, and plead for pardon, since I, un-
luckily, left you in a puddle; and I sincerely hope
you'll never be in such a pickle again.

*Luc.* Stand away, you brute!

*Olla.* Sir Robert, I hope you won't withdraw your
friendship—and it would give a mortification to be
cut off from your custom.

*Sir Rob.* Oh, master Ollapod, your little foibles
are like your small quantities of magnesia; they give
no great nausea, and do neither harm nor good.

*Olla.* Come, that's very well; very well indeed!
Thank you, good Sir, I owe you one—I'll stay, and
he'll ask me to dinner. [*Aside.*]

*Sir Rob.* And, what are you saying, there, to Miss
Worthington, Frederick?

*Fred.* Telling her what good cheer there is in
Blackberry Hall, uncle—and what a worthy gentleman at the head of the table, where I am going to
have the pleasure to lead her.

*Sir Rob.* You are devilish ready to do the honours;
isn't he, Mr. Worthington?

*Worth.* To do honour to the human heart, Sir, I
have found him very ready.

*Sir Rob.* And have you found him so very ready
to do honour to the heart, Miss Worthington?

*Emily.* Yes, indeed I have, Sir.

*Sir Rob.* I begin to perceive it. I'm a strange old fellow—fond of argument, they say. But I have so little time left, now, in this world, that some of my arguments are a little shorter than they used to be. When I was hobbling over the stile, after Frederick, there,—and thought the dog might be shivered to atoms—I made a determination in my own mind, if he happened to survive, that he, and your daughter —What's your name, young lady?

*Emily.* Emily, Sir.

*Sir Rob.* Ha! a pretty name enough—that he and Emily shou'd make a happy couple.

*Worth.* Never, Sir.

*Sir Rob.* That's a plump *negatur.* We'll argue that point, if you please.

*Worth.* My child, Sir Robert, has heard my opinions very lately; and hearing the opinions of a friend, she adopts them.

*Sir Rob.* Does she? Then she's as little like Humphrey Dobbins in her mind, as she is in her features.

*Worth.* To you it may, now, be necessary to say that I am poorer even than poor—but observe, I disdain all solicitations—This very day I have been apprised—

*Sir Rob.* Oh, I know what you mean—The bond for five hundred pounds.

*Worth.* How came you apprised of that bond, Sir? [*Rather haughtily.*]

*Sir Rob.* I have paid it.

*Worth.* Paid it!

*Sir Rob.* Yes—while Frederick was loading his pistols, in the next room, to come to the field, here.

*Worth.* You astonish me!

*Sir Rob.* Why so? I happen to be Sheriff of the County; and, as all writs are returnable to me, a scrubbyish fellow ask'd me to sign one against you. I thought it might be as well not to lock up a worthy man, in a scurvy room, just as I had ask'd him, from no common motives, to sit down to my table—so, I drew upon my bankers, instead of John Doe, and

Richard Roe,—and you may reimburse me at your leisure.

*Fred.* My dear, dear uncle! you have been before me here!

*Sir Rob.* You rogue, if your fortune could serve you as well as your legs, I believe you'd have been before me here, too.

*Worth.* I know not what to say to you, Sir Robert.

*Sir Rob.* Confess you're a damn'd bad physiognomist, and I'm content. Say a man's countenance may a little belye his nature;—though, as Sheriff of the County, I own I am head of the bum-bailiffs.

*Worth.* I shall never be able to repay you this debt, Sir, but by long and miserable instalments.

*Sir Rob.* You shall give me security.

*Worth.* I wish it.—Any in my power.

*Sir Rob.* Miss Emily, pray come here—Frederick, you dog, come on the other side of me. Let me appoint you two trustees for a bond Mr. Worthington shall give me—a bond of family alliance—fulfil your charge punctually, and Heaven prosper you in your obligations. Mr. Worthington, what say you?

*Worth.* You overwhelm me—I cannot speak.

[FREDERICK *embraces* EMILY.

*Sir Rob.* The trustees are dumb too :—but I see they are embracing the obligations, pretty willingly.

*Olla.* A marriage between the young ones. I hope I may be in favour with the family nine months hence.

*Luc.* Sir Robert, I rejoice at the alliance. The Brambles came in with the Conqueror, and are no disgrace to the Mac Tabs.

*Sir Rob.* I haven't the honour to know exactly who you may be, Madam; but I thank you. But, damn it!—our dinner will be waiting—Make one of the party, if you please, Ollapod.

*Olla.* I'll attack your mutton with all my heart, Sir Robert. I knew he'd ask me to dinner.

*Fred.* Come, Emily! let me lead you to a house,

where our days may be long, be happy. You look doubtingly.

*Emily.* No, indeed—When my father doubted, I have doubted—but I can read his eyes—as he, I own, not long since, read my heart. You have been my preserver, and I can't help feeling gratitude.

*Sir Rob.* Love, you mean, you little devil ! Frederick, we'll have Job a grandfather before he can get from Russia.

*Fred.* My dear uncle, your hand—Mr. Worthington, suffer me to press yours. Emily, you have my heart. And may hearts, when unvitiated by the world, meet the happiness I expect, and the approbation of the virtuous !

# EPILOGUE.

*Olla.* DULL Care, avaunt! all, here, are now content

*Sir Rob.* Hold—that admits, perhaps, of argument,

Some may be sicken'd here——

*Luc.* But, how to know?

*Olla.* Their pulses must be felt before we go.

*Sir Rob.* Their pulses! That by you were better done.

*Olla.* That's very well—thank you—I owe you one.

Hold up your heads, pray.   Hum—ha! 'gad they smile!

The Patients don't seem troubled with much bile.

I dose men's spirits to their proper pitch;

As Cornet, every lady I bewitch:

*Luc.* Not, when you leave a lady in a ditch.

*Worth.* As father, I each father's favour court—

*Emily.* As daughter, I from daughters ask support.

*Olla.* Apothecaries, cheer me with your bounty.

*Sir Rob.* Bum-bailiffs, Me, as sheriff of the county.

*Fred.* I deprecate the cruel Critick's stabs;

*Luc.* And I—by all the blood of the Mac Tabs!

*Worth.* And if, to-night, my efforts shou'd succeed,

Then the *Poor Gentleman* feels rich indeed.

THE END.

PLAYS printed for LONGMAN, HURST, REES, and ORME, No. 39, Paternoster-Row.

1. ALMAHIDE and HAMET, a Tragedy in five Acts; to which is prefixed a LETTER to JOHN PHILIP KEMBLE, Esq. on Dramatic Composition. By BENJAMIN HEATH MALKIN, Esq. M. A. Handsomely printed by Bensley. Royal 8vo. Price 6s. in boards.

2. MARY STEWART, QUEEN of SCOTS, an Historical Drama, 8vo. Price 4s. sewed.

"The Life and Death of Mary Queen of Scots has been rendered so familiar to every Briton by poets, historians, and even dramatists, that to give an air of novelty to the incidents of her ill-fated story, or to impart additional interest to them by poetic language, and stage effect, is a task of no easy attainment; the limitations of history become despotic restraints upon the freedom of imagination.

"By the present anonymous writer, much ingenuity, however, is shewn in the management of his drama, and much characteristic spirit is displayed in pourtraying the rival Queens."

*Monthly Mirror, Jan. 1802.*

3. WALLENSTEIN, an Historical Drama, in two Parts, Translated from the German of Frederick Schiller, by S. T. COLERIDGE. In one volume 8vo. embellished with an elegant Engraving of Wallenstein. Price 8s. sewed.

4. SHAKSPEARE's OTHELLO, the Moor of Venice, a Tragedy, revised by J. P. KEMBLE, and now first published as it is acted at the Theatre Royal in Covent-Garden, 8vo. 2s. It is intended to publish the whole of Shakspeare's acting plays uniformly with this.

5. ———— KING JOHN, an Historical Play, revised by Ditto, 2s.

6. KING HENRY the Eighth, an Historical Play, revised by Ditto.

7. DELAYS AND BLUNDERS, a Comedy in five Acts, by Mr. REYNOLDS, price 2s. 6d.

8. MOUNTAINEERS, a Play by Ditto, 2s.

9. SPEED THE PLOUGH, a Comedy, by Mr. MORTON, 2s.

10. ZORINSKI, a Play by Ditto, 2s.

11. The WAY TO GET MARRIED, a Comedy, by Ditto, 2s.

12. The CURE FOR THE HEART-ACHE, a Comedy, by Ditto, 2s.

13. SECRETS WORTH KNOWING, a Comedy, by Ditto, 2s.

14. FOLLY AS IT FLIES, a Comedy, by Mr. REYNOLDS, 2s. 6d.

15. LIFE, a Comedy, by Ditto, 2s.

16. MANAGEMENT, a Comedy, by Ditto, 2s.

17. LAUGH WHEN YOU CAN, a Comedy, by Ditto, 2s.

18. The DRAMATIST, a Comedy, by Ditto, 2s.

19. NOTORIETY, a Comedy, by Ditto, 2s.

20. HOW TO GROW RICH, a Comedy, by Ditto, 2s.

21. The RAGE, a Comedy, by Ditto, 2s.

22. SPECULATION, a Comedy, by Ditto, 2s.

23. WERTER, a Tragedy, by Ditto, 2s.

24. The POINT OF HONOUR, a Play, by Mr. C. KEMBLE, 2s.

JOYCE GOLD, PRINTER, SHOE-LANE.

CPSIA information can be obtained
at www.ICGtesting.com
Printed in the USA
BVHW051045210721
612411BV00012B/3644